# *THE OFFICIAL WATFORD FOOTBALL CLUB QUIZ BOOK*

# THE OFFICIAL WATFORD FOOTBALL CLUB QUIZ BOOK

*COMPILED BY CHRIS COWLIN*
*FOREWORD BY GRAHAM TAYLOR OBE*

APEX PUBLISHING LTD

First published in 2007, Updated and reprinted in 2007 by
**Apex Publishing Ltd**
PO Box 7086, Clacton on Sea, Essex, CO15 5WN, England

**www.apexpublishing.co.uk**

**British Library Cataloguing-in-Publication Data**
**A catalogue record for this book**
**is available from the British Library**

ISBN 1-904444-85-7          978-1904444-85-5

Typeset in 10.5pt Chianti BdIt Win95BT

Cover Design:  Andrew Macey

Printed and bound in Great Britain

The club badge was kindly supplied by Watford FC

**This book is an official product of Watford FC**

**Author's Note:**
Please can you contact me - ChrisCowlin@btconnect.com - if you find any mistakes/errors in this book as I would like to put them right on any future reprints. I would also like to hear from Watford fans who have enjoyed the test! **Visit Chris' website: www.ChrisCowlin.com**

*This book is dedicated to*
*my family*
*who are always there when needed most*
*and*
*Graham Taylor OBE - a true footballing legend!*

# FOREWORD

So here is your first question: Name the happiest ten years in the life of Graham Taylor, former manager of Watford Football Club?

Anyone who got that wrong surely cannot be a true Hornets supporter. 1977 to 1987 is of course the correct answer.

I know I do not have to write this, but even all these years on I still get a wonderful warm feeling when I reel these facts off:

* 1977/78 - Fourth Division Champions
* 1978/79 - Promotion from the Third Division
* 1981/82 - Promotion from the Second Division
* 1982/83 - Runners-up in the First Division
* 1983/84 - UEFA Cup participation and FA Cup Finalists.

Add to that both a Football League Cup and an FA Cup semi-final appearance and a lowest position ever of 12th in the First Division. Some story eh?!

But for me the biggest achievement was what the club stood for off the pitch: a family, community-orientated club that in difficult 'hooligan' football times gave a lead as to how clubs could operate; the first all-seated family enclosure; the first standing family enclosure; the first club to have written into their players' contracts a clause to commit themselves to so many hours' work and appearances in and with the community of Watford and the surrounding areas. This club belonged to the town of Watford. It was special and so it will remain special to me until my dying day. Thanks to you all.

For every sale of a copy of this book £1 will be donated to the charity Sense, which supports and aids people who are both deaf and blind. Try to imagine that 'thank you' for your contribution.

I hope you enjoy the 1,000 questions in this book that Chris has compiled. I thought I knew a lot about Watford Football Club, but I was still stuck on a few. The questions cover *everything - great matches, players, transfers, top goalscorers, managers, positions in the League and much, much more. This book is guaranteed to provide hours of enjoyment for any Watford fan.*

*Best wishes*

**Graham Taylor OBE**
*Watford Football Club (Manager 1977-1987 & 1996-2001)*

# INTRODUCTION

I would first of all like to thank Graham Taylor for writing the foreword to this book. I am very grateful for his help on this project and was truly delighted when he agreed to write a few words as I am a big Graham Taylor fan.

I would also like to thank all the past and present players of Watford Football Club for their comments and reviews (which can be found at the back of the book).

I am honoured to donate £1 from the sale of each book to Sense, which is a registered charity - **www.sense.org.uk**. Sense is the UK's largest organisation dedicated to children and adults who are deafblind or have associated disabilities. This charity was Graham Taylor's choice, as he helps them on a regular basis, and now, having read what they do it and knowing more about their work, I would love to help the charity again in the future as well as through this book.

I would like to thank Vanessa Langford, Ben Parry and Tony Best for their help and support in creating this book. I would also like to say a BIG thank you to Scott Field and Sarah Winning at Watford Football Club for their help and advice during the book's compilation.

I really hope you enjoy this book. Hopefully it should bring back some wonderful memories!

In closing, I would like to thank all my friends and family for encouraging me to complete this project, especially John and Barbie Knight.

*Chris Cowlin.*

*Best wishes*
*Chris Cowlin*

# THE CLUB - RECORDS & HISTORY

1.      What is Watford's nickname?

2.      In what year was the club formed as Watford Rovers?

3.      Watford's record signing was Allan Nielsen for £2.25
        million. From which club did Watford sign him in 2000?

4.      In what year did Watford join the Football League -
        1920, 1930 or 1940?

5.      Which player scored a record 42 goals in a season,
        during 1959/1960?

6.      Which former player holds the record for the most
        appearances and goals scored at Watford?

7.      In February 1969 Watford recorded their record
        attendance, against which team?

8.      Who has been the most capped England player whilst at
        Watford, with 31 caps?

9.      Watford recorded their record League victory in
        September 1982 against Sunderland. What was the
        score?

10.     In what year did Watford move to Vicarage Road - 1912,
        1922 or 1932?

# LUTHER BLISSETT

11. In what year was Luther born in Jamaica - 1956, 1957 or 1958?

12. In December 1983 Luther scored a hat-trick for England in a 9-0 win, against which country?

13. How many League goals has Luther scored for Watford in his career - 118, 138 or 158?

14. How many spells at Watford did Luther have - 2, 3 or 4?

15. For which Italian team did Luther play during 1983/1984 only for him to return to Vicarage Road for the following season?

16. In April 1975 Luther made his Watford debut against which team - Bury, Birmingham City or Barnsley?

17. Viv Anderson was the first black player to play for England, but what was Luther the first player to do?

18. Which Watford manager handed Luther his debut at Vicarage Road?

19. How many England caps did Luther win for his country, scoring three goals?

20. In what position did Luther play?

# MANAGERS

*Match up the former Watford manager with the period he was manager at the club*

| | | |
|---|---|---|
| 21. | Ray Lewington | 1952-1955 |
| 22. | Glenn Roeder | 1929-1937 |
| 23. | Mike Keen | 1990-1993 |
| 24. | Len Goulden | 2002-2005 |
| 25. | Steve Perryman | 1977-1987 |
| 26. | Graham Taylor | 1993-1996 |
| 27. | Eddie Hapgood | 2001-2002 |
| 28. | Graham Taylor | 1973-1977 |
| 29. | Neil McBain | 1948-1950 |
| 30. | Gianluca Vialli | 1996-2001 |

# GRAHAM TAYLOR OBE

31.   Which team was Graham appointed manager of in 1972?

32.   In what year was Graham appointed Watford manager for the first time - 1975, 1976 or 1977?

33.   Graham was appointed as England manager in 1990. Which team did England face in his first match in charge at Wembley in a 1-0 win?

34.   Which honour did Graham acheive in 2002 for his services to football?

35.   Which catchphrase is Graham most known for saying during his England manager days?

36.   Which Midlands team did Graham manage between 1994 and 1995?

37.   For which team did Graham play between 1962 and 1968?

38.   For how many games was Graham in charge of England during his England manager career between 1990 and 1993?

39.   When Graham left Watford as manager in 2001, who took over as Hornets manager?

40.   In what year was Graham born - 1944, 1945 or 1946?

# WHERE DID THEY GO? - 1

*Match up the player with the club they joined after leaving Watford*

| | | |
|---|---|---|
| 41. | Andy Hessenthaler | West Bromwich Albion |
| 42. | Hameur Bouazza | Luton Town |
| 43. | Neil Redfearn | Norwich City |
| 44. | David Connolly | Walsall |
| 45. | Matthew Spring | Gillingham |
| 46. | Clint Easton | Cardiff City |
| 47. | Paul Devlin | Feyenoord |
| 48. | Neil Cox | Fulham |
| 49. | Paul Robinson | Bristol Rovers |
| 50. | Gary Penrice | Oldham Athletic |

# STEVE SHERWOOD

51.    In which year was Steve born - 1953, 1954 or 1955?

52.    In what position did Steve play during his playing career?

53.    How many goals did Steve score for Watford in his career?

54.    In which year did Steve make his Watford debut?

55.    How many League appearances did Steve make for the Hornets during his career?

56.    In how many of Watford's UEFA Cup matches during 1983/1984 did Steve play?

57.    Steve was the only player to be playing for Watford throughout the first spell of which Watford manager?

58.    What was Steve's brother John Sherwood famous for?

59.    Which team did Steve join when he left Vicarge Road in 1987?

60.    Against which Scottish team did Steve play his testimonial in 1987?

# PLAYER OF THE YEAR - 1

*Match up the player with the season in*
*which he won Player of the Year*

| | | |
|---|---|---|
| 61. | 1972/1973 | Wilf Rostron |
| 62. | 1974/1975 | Ross Jenkins |
| 63. | 1976/1977 | Tony Coton |
| 64. | 1978/1979 | David James |
| 65. | 1980/1981 | John McClelland |
| 66. | 1982/1983 | Andy Rankin |
| 67. | 1984/1985 | Glyn Hodges |
| 68. | 1986/1987 | Steve Sims |
| 69. | 1988/1989 | Keith Mercer |
| 70. | 1990/1991 | Andy Rankin |

# PREMIER LEAGUE 1999/2000

71. Against which team did Watford record their first League win in a 1-0 away match on 14 August 1999 with Tommy Mooney scoring?

72. Who scored the only goal in a 1-0 win on the last day of the season at Vicarage Road against Coventry City?

73. How many League games did Watford win during the season - 6, 8 or 10?

74. Who was the manager in charge during the season?

75. Which player scored the only goal in the 1-0 home win against Chelsea in September 1999?

76. Which team did Watford beat 1-0 in March 2000 with Allan Smart scoring the goal - Sheffield United, Everton or Sheffield Wednesday?

77. Can you name the two goalscorers that scored against Southampton in the 3-2 home win in December 1999?

78. Can you name the only player to start in all 38 games?

79. Which Iceland forward finished as Watford's highest League scorer with 6 League goals?

80. Watford beat Bradford City 1-0 in August 1999, but which Hornet scored?

# MATCH THE YEAR - 1

*Match up the year with Watford's achievement*

| 81. | FA Cup Runners-Up | 1978 |
|-----|-------------------|------|
| 82. | League Cup Semi-Finalists | 1983 |
| 83. | Division Three Champions | 1999 |
| 84. | League Cup Semi-Finalists | 1998 |
| 85. | FA Cup Semi-Finalists | 2006 |
| 86. | Division Four Champions | 1969 |
| 87. | Division One Runners-Up | 1984 |
| 88. | Division Two Champions | 2004 |
| 89. | Championship Play-off Winners | 2003 |
| 90. | First Division Play-off Winners | 1979 |

# DARREN WARD

91.   In which year was Darren born in London - 1976, 1977 or 1978?

92.   Darren made his Watford debut in 1996 against which side, drawing 0-0?

93.   How many goals, in all competitions, did Darren score for Watford during his career?

94.   Darren scored his first goal for Watford in May 2000 against which Premier League team, drawing 1-1 away from home?

95.   In what position did Darren play for Watford?

96.   Against which team did Darren score in a 3-0 away League Cup, win with Tommy Smith and Heidar Helguson also scoring?

97.   Darren scored for Watford in a 3-2 win against Sheffield Wednesday at Hillsborough. Can you name the two other Watford scorers?

98.   Which London team did Darren sign for in 2006?

99.   During 1999/2000 Darren spent time on loan at which London club?

100.  When Darren left Watford in 2001, which team did he sign for?

# TOP LEAGUE GOALSCORERS IN A SEASON

*Match up the player with the season in which he was top League goalscorer*

101.  1996/1997        Heidar Helguson, 6 goals

102.  1997/1998        Tommy Smith, 11 goals

103.  1998/1999        Tommy Mooney, 19 goals

104.  1999/2000        Heidar Helguson, 16 goals

105.  2000/2001        Peter Kennedy, 11 goals

106.  2001/2002        Marlon King, 21 goals

107.  2002/2003        Tommy Mooney, 13 goals

108.  2003/2004        Gifton Noel-Williams, 10 goals

109.  2004/2005        Scott Fitzgerald, 10 goals

110.  2005/2006        Heidar Helguson, 11 goals

# THE UEFA CUP - 1983/1984

111.  Who scored Watford's first ever goal in European competition?

112.  Who was the Watford manager during this cup run?

113.  Which Hornets captain led Watford out against Kaiserslautern in their first competitive game in European competition?

114.  How many goals did Watford score in their 6 UEFA cup matches - 6, 8 or 10?

115.  Which player scored a brace against Kaiserslautern at Vicarage Road in the 3-0 home win?

116.  Can you name 7 of the starting 11 that played in their first ever UEFA game?

117.  Can you name 2 of the only 4 players that started all 6 UEFA cup matches?

118.  Which German team scored an own goal, credited to Watford in a 3-0 win?

119.  Which player scored after coming on as substitute against Sparta Prague at Vicarage Road?

120.  Which team knocked Watford out of the competition by defeating them 3-2 at Vicarage Road and 4-0 away from home?

# WHO AM I?

121. I made my debut for Watford in 1990, I am a goalkeeper, and in 2006 I signed for Portsmouth.

122. I was born in Jamaica in 1963, I made 79 caps for England, and when I left Vicarage Road I signed for Liverpool.

123. I signed for Watford in July 1996 on a free transfer, and my previous clubs include Colchester United, Luton Town and Sunderland.

124. I finshed as Watford's top League goalscorer during 1983/1984 with 20 goals.

125. I was born in 1944, I was appointed Watford manager in 1977 and I resigned as England manager in 1993.

126. I made my debut for Watford during the 1983/1984 season, and made 3 League and 2 UEFA appearances during this season.

127. I signed for Watford for £1.5 million from Wigan Athletic in 2006, and I scored on my debut against Everton.

128. I joined Watford in 1985 from Arsenal, and before playing for the Gunners I played for Ipswich Town.

129. I finshed as Watford's highest scorer during 1984/1985 with 21 League, 6 FA Cup and 1 League Cup goals.

130. I was born in Singapore in 1962, I made my Watford debut in September 1980, and I left Vicarage Road in 1987 to join Derby County.

# PROMOTION TO DIVISION ONE
# - 1981/1982

131.    How many of the 42 League games did Watford win
        - 13, 23 or 33?

132.    In what position did Watford finish - 2nd, 3rd or 4th?

133.    Which Hornets manager led Watford to this success?

134.    Can you name the only two players who started all
        42 League matches?

135.    Name the club's highest scorer with 19 League goals
        in 40 matches?

136.    Watford recorded their biggest win in January 1982,
        the game ending 6-1, against which team?

137.    How many League goals did Watford score in the 42
        League matches - 66, 76 or 86?

138.    In March 1982 Watford beat which London team 4-0
        at Vicarage Road - Fulham, Tottenham Hotspur or
        Queens Park Rangers?

139.    Can you name the two players who finished the season
        with 13 League goals apiece?

140.    How many League goals did Jan Lohman score for
        Watford - 2, 4 or 6?

# TOM WALLEY

141. In what year was Tom born - 1941, 1943 or 1945?

142. Which manager gave Tom his Watford debut?

143. In what position did Tom play for Watford?

144. How many goals did Tom score in his first season at Watford, 1966/1967?

145. Which country did Tom represent at under-23 and full international level?

146. In how many League games did Tom appear for Watford - 217, 317 or 417?

147. From which London team did Watford sign Tom?

148. Which role at Vicarage Road did Tom take between 1988 and 1990?

149. How many League goals did Tom score for Watford during his career?

150. Which award did Tom win whilst at Watford in 1970/1971?

# PAT JENNINGS

151. *In what year was Pat born - 1943, 1944 or 1945?*

152. *How many games did Pat play for Watford - 52, 152 or 252?*

153. *How much did Watford pay for Pat in May 1963 when he signed from Newry Town?*

154. *Which Watford manager was in charge during Pat's first and only full season at the club, 1963/1964?*

155. *Pat made his international debut whilst a Watford player, against which United Kingdom based country?*

156. *What was Pat awarded in 1976 for his services to football?*

157. *In 1977 which London team did Pat join?*

158. *In what position did Pat play during his playing days?*

159. *For which country did Pat win 119 international caps?*

160. *When Pat left Watford which club did he sign for?*

# HAT-TRICK HEROES

*Match up the player with the match in which
he scored a hat-trick*

161.     *v. Port Vale (Home)*
       *Apr 1996, League, 5-2 win*        **Tommy Mooney**

162.     *v. Grimsby Town (Home)*
       *Apr 1996, League, 6-3 win*        **Darren Bazeley**

163.     *v. Grimsby Town (Home)*
       *Apr 1996, League, 6-3 win*        **Ross Jenkins**

164.     *v. Norwich City (Home)*
       *Dec 2001, League, 4-0 win*        **Maurice Johnston**

165.     *v. Southend United (Away)*
       *Feb 1995, League, 4-0 win*        **Ross Jenkins**

166.     *v. Bolton Wanderers (Home)*
       *Oct 1993, League, 4-3 win*        **Craig Ramage**

167.     *v. Blackpool (Home)*
       *Aug 1978, League, 5-1 win*        **David Connolly**

168.     *v. Dagenham (Home)*
       *Nov 1978, FA Cup 1st Round, 3-0 win*        **Luther Blissett**

169.     *v. Wolves (Away)*
       *Dec 1983, League, 5-0 win*        **David Connolly**

170.     *v. Notts County (Home)*
       *Mar 1983, FA Cup 6th round, 5-3 win*        **Gary Porter**

# DAMIEN FRANCIS

171. In what year was Damien born - 1977, 1979 or 1981?

172. When Damien signed for Watford, which squad number was he given?

173. Which Hornets manager signed Damien for Watford?

174. Damien scored on his Watford League debut in a 2-1 defeat, against which team?

175. Which East Anglian side did Damien play for between 2003 and 2005?

176. How much did Watford pay for Damien?

177. Which club did Damien play for and start his career at (between 1997 and 2003)?

178. Against which North-East based team did Damien score in the League Cup in November 2006?

179. Against which team did Damien score in a 2-1 home defeat on 26 August 2006?

180. What nationality is Damien?

# MAURICE JOHNSTON

181. Maurice made his Watford debut in November 1983, against which team in a 4-1 defeat?

182. Where was Maurice born in 1963 - Manchester, London or Glasgow?

183. During 1983/1984 Maurice made 29 League appearances for Watford, scoring how many goals?

184. Can you name the French club that Maurice played for between 1987 and 1989?

185. Maurice won 38 caps for Scotland, scoring how many goals?

186. How many League goals did Maurice score for Watford in his 38 League appearances for the club?

187. From which Scottish team did Watford sign Maurice in November 1983?

188. Which Hornets manager signed Maurice for Watford in 1983?

189. Can you name the English top-flight team that Maurice played for between 1991 and 1993?

190. Maurice transferred from Watford to which Scottish club in October 1984?

# STEVE PALMER

191.    In what year was Steve born - 1966, 1968 or 1970?

192.    Steve signed for Watford in November 1995, from which East Anglian team?

193.    In what position did Steve play for Watford?

194.    Against which team did Steve make his Watford League debut in September 1995, in a 3-2 win?

195.    During 1996/1997 Steve scored twice for Watford, against which two sides?

196.    Against which East Anglian team did Steve score the equaliser in a 1-1 draw in December 1998?

197.    Which team did Steve play for between 2004 and 2006?

198.    How many League goals did Steve score in his Watford career - 4, 6 or 8?

199.    Steve scored his last goal for Watford in November 2000 in a 3-2 home defeat to which side?

200.    In July 2001 Steve left Vicarage Road and signed for which London team?

# 1990s

201. What was the score when Watford visited Millwall in December 1991 in Division 2?

202. Which player signed for Watford in 1994 after signing from Baldock Town?

203. Which forward signed from Nottingham Forest in 1997?

204. Following on from the previous question, against which team did he score a brace in a 4-1 home win in November 1997, with Richard Johnson and Ronny Rosenthal also scoring for the Hornets?

205. Watford recorded their first ever Premier League win in August 1999, winning 1-0 against which team?

206. Can you name the three Watford managers that managed the club in 1990?

207. Which player won Watford 'Young Player of the Year' during 1990/1991?

208. Which 2 players scored the goals in the 2-0, last game of the season win away against Crystal Palace in May 1994?

209. Who did Watford buy from Coventry City in 1992, only for him to leave Vicarage Road in 1994 for Chelsea?

210. Who scored the goals in Watford's last game of 1999, a 3-2 home win against Southampton in the Premier League?

# ANDY RANKIN

211. In what year was Andy born - 1940, 1942 or 1944?

212. From which team did Watford sign Andy in 1971?

213. How much did Watford pay for Andy?

214. Andy made his debut during 1971/1972. How many League appearances did he make in his first season at Watford?

215. Which manager signed Andy for Watford?

216. Which team did Andy sign for when he left Vicarage Road?

217. Can you name the three managers that Andy played under at Watford?

218. Which country did Andy represent at under-23 level?

219. One Watford goalkeeper has played more games in goal than Andy. Can you name him?

220. How many League appearances did Andy make for Watford - 199, 299 or 399?

# BIG WINS - 1

*Match up Watford's winning score with the match
in which it was achieved*

| 221. | v. Stockport County (Home) FA Cup 3rd Round, January 2007 | 7-2 |
|---|---|---|
| 222. | v. Southampton (Home) League Cup 4th Round, November 2004 | 4-0 |
| 223. | v. Coventry City (Home) League, August 2002 | 6-3 |
| 224. | v. Grimsby Town (Home) League, November 2000 | 4-1 |
| 225. | v. Blackpool (Home) League, November 1997 | 5-2 |
| 226. | v. Grimsby Town (Home) League, April 1996 | 8-0 |
| 227. | v. Southend United (Away) League, February 1995 | 5-2 |
| 228. | v. Bristol City (Home) League, May 1992 | 4-1 |
| 229. | v. Bradford City (Home) League, December 1989 | 5-2 |
| 230. | v. Darlington (Home) League Cup 2nd Round, October 1987 | 4-0 |

# WATFORD V. CHELSEA

231.    By what score did Watford beat Chelsea when the sides met on 18 September 1999, their first encounter in the Premier League?

232.    Following on from the previous question, which player scored for Watford?

233.    What was the score when the sides met in the 1986/1987 FA Cup at Vicarage Road?

234.    Which player scored the only goal in the 1-0 Watford win in February 1981 away from home?

235.    Can you name the three goalscorers when Watford won 3-1 in April 1987 at Vicarage Road?

236.    In February 1987 the Hornets beat Chelsea 1-0 in the 4th round of the FA Cup. Who scored?

237.    Which players scored for the Hornets in the 2-2 home FA Cup draw in January 2004?

238.    What was the score when Watford beat Chelsea in Division One in May 1986?

239.    True or False: Watford beat Chelsea 3-2 at Stamford Bridge, their first ever meeting in Division One in October 1984.

240.    Which three players scored Watford's goals in the 3-1 home win in September 1985 in Division One?

# FA CUP SEMI-FINALISTS 2003

241. Which team did Watford beat 2-0 in the 3rd round?

242. Following on from the previous questions, which two players scored the goals?

243. Which team did the Hornets play in the 5th round, winning 1-0, with Tommy Smith scoring?

244. Watford beat Burnley in the quarter-finals. What was the score?

245. Following on from the previous questions, which Watford players scored the goals?

246. Which team did Watford meet in the semi-final?

247. Following on from the previous question, what was the score in the match?

248. Following on from the previous question, which Watford player scored?

249. At which stadium was the semi-final held?

250. Which Watford player scored the only goal in the 4th round 1-0 home win against West Bromwich Albion?

# THE LEAGUE CUP

**251.** Which substitute came from the bench to score two goals in the 3-2 away win in October 1994 against Spurs?

**252.** In September 2006 with which team did Watford draw 0-0 in the 2nd round, and then beat 6-5 on penalties?

**253.** What was the score when Watford first met Middlesbrough in the League Cup in October 1999?

**254.** Which Midlands side did Watford beat 2-1 during September 2005 at Vicarage Road in Round 2, with Clarke Carlisle scoring twice, the 2nd goal in extra time?

**255.** Who scored the only winning goal in a 1-0 win against Bournemouth in August 2003?

**256.** In October 2006 Watford beat which team 2-1, with Tamas Priskin and Ashley Young scoring?

**257.** In September 2000 Watford beat Cheltenham 3-0 in the 1st round, 2nd leg. Which three players scored?

**258.** What was the score when Watford met Swindon Town at the County Ground in August 1997?

**259.** Against which Essex team did Craig Ramage score the only winning goal in a 1-0 win in August 1994 in the 1st round, 2nd leg?

**260.** Which two Watford players scored the goals in the 2-2 home draw against Newcastle United during November 2006?

# JOHN BARNES

261. In which country was John born in 1963?

262. In what year was John given his Watford League debut?

263. Following on from the previous question, can you name the team that John made his debut against as a 17-year-old in a 1-1 draw?

264. During 1982/1983 John started all 42 League games for Watford, scoring how many goals - 6, 8 or 10?

265. For which club did John play between 1997 and 1999?

266. How many League goals did John score for Watford in his career - 55, 65 or 75?

267. Which Scottish team was John made manager of in 1999, only to leave in 2000?

268. When John left Watford in 1987, which club did he join?

269. How many League goals did John score in his final season, 1986/1987, at Vicarage Road?

270. John won 79 England caps for his country, scoring how many goals - 9, 11 or 13?

# LES TAYLOR

271.    In what position did Les play for Watford?

272.    From which club did Watford sign Les?

273.    During 1981/1982 Les made 42 League appearances for the Hornets, scoring how many goals - 4, 6 or 8?

274.    Les played for Watford in the 1984 FA Cup Final, but what was extra special for him on the day?

275.    Les made his Watford League debut in November 1980, in a 1-0 home defeat against which club?

276.    How many League goals did Les score in his Watford career - 3, 13 or 23?

277.    Which manager signed Les for Watford and was still manager when Les left Vicarage Road in 1985?

278.    In what year was Les born in North Shields - 1946, 1956 or 1966?

279.    How many League appearances did Les make for Watford - 132, 152 or 172?

280.    In October 1986 Les left Vicarage Road and signed for which club?

# 1970s

281. Who finished as top League scorer with 11 goals during 1974/1975?

282. During 1978/1979 Watford bought which player for a record £175,000?

283. Who finished top League scorer with 22 goals during 1976/1977?

284. Only one player played in all 46 League matches during 1972/1973. Can you name him?

285. Who finsihed top League scorer with only 6 goals during 1972/1973?

286. In what position did Watford finish in the League during 1976/1977 - 3rd, 5th or 7th?

287. Who won the first Watford Observer Player of the Season award in 1972/1973?

288. Ross Jenkins finished top goalscorer during 1978/1979 with how many goals, in all competitions?

289. How much did a match-day programme cost during 1971/1972?

290. Who managed Watford between 1973 and 1977?

# STEVE SIMS

291.  In 1978 Steve signed for Watford, from which side?

292.  Which manager signed Steve for Watford in 1978?

293.  In December 1978 Steve made his debut against which Essex based team?

294.  Graham Taylor signed Steve for which future club for both of them?

295.  How many League games did Steve play for Watford - 171, 211 or 251?

296.  How much did Watford pay for Steve, a Division 3 record in 1978?

297.  How many League goals did Steve score for Watford in his career?

298.  How many League goals did Steve score in his first season at Vicarage Road?

299.  Which country did Steve represent at under-21 and 'B' level?

300.  Which team did Steve leave Watford to join in September 1984, returning to Watford for a second spell in October 1986?

# PAT RICE

301.    In what year did Pat join Watford?

302.    How many goals did Pat score for Watford in his career, in all competitions?

303.    Pat won youth, under-23 and full caps for his country, but what nationality is he?

304.    What position did Pat play during his playing days?

305.    From which London club did Watford sign Pat?

306.    How many League games did Pat win for Watford - 52, 112 or 152?

307.    Which Watford manager brought Pat to Vicarage Road?

308.    Which position did Pat take up at Highbury in 1984, on leaving Watford?

309.    How many full international caps did Pat win for his country?

310.    In what year was Pat born - 1945, 1947 or 1949?

# GLENN ROEDER

**311.** Glenn was appointed Watford manager in 1993, but in what year did he leave that position?

**312.** For which London team did Glenn play between 1973 and 1978?

**313.** In what year did Glenn sign for Watford as a player?

**314.** In what year was Glenn born - 1950, 1955 or 1960?

**315.** Which London team did Glenn manage between 2001 and 2003?

**316.** How many League goals did Glenn score for Watford during 1989/1990?

**317.** Which team did Glenn manage during 1992/1993?

**318.** Apart from Watford and the club in Q312, which two other clubs did Glenn play for during his playing career?

**319.** How many League games did Glenn win as manager of Watford - 19, 29 or 39?

**320.** Which top-flight team was Glenn appointed manager of in February 2006?

# SQUAD NUMBERS - 2007/2008

*Match up the player with his squad number
for the 2007/2008 season*

| | | |
|---|---|---|
| 321. | Lloyd Doyley | 21 |
| 322. | Damien Francis | 18 |
| 323. | Lee Williamson | 25 |
| 324. | Jobi McAnuff | 7 |
| 325. | Gareth Williams | 35 |
| 326. | Gavin Mahon | 14 |
| 327. | Mart Poom | 11 |
| 328. | Nathan Ellington | 12 |
| 329. | Tommy Smith | 8 |
| 330. | John O'Toole | 1 |

# CAPS FOR MY COUNTRY

*Match up the player with the number of caps*
*earned while playing for his country*

| | | |
|---|---|---|
| 331. | Chris Powell | 31 Wales Caps |
| 332. | John Barnes | 15 Wales Caps |
| 333. | Kenny Jackett | 119 Northern Ireland Caps |
| 334. | Tony Coton | 77 Canada Caps |
| 335. | Luther Blissett | 2 England Caps |
| 336. | Mark Watson | 79 England Caps |
| 337. | Iwan Roberts | 5 England Caps |
| 338. | David Bardsley | 63 Northern Ireland Caps |
| 339. | Gerry Armstrong | 14 England Caps |
| 340. | Pat Jennings | 1 England B Cap |

# DIVISION FOUR CHAMPIONS
# - 1977/1978

341. Watford won the title by 11 points, but which Essex based team finished runners-up to the Hornets?

342. Who was the only player to start in all 46 League matches?

343. Ross Jenkins finished as Watford's highest League scorer, with how many goals?

344. How many players were used by Watford during the season success - 18, 21 or 23?

345. Which player scored the club's 2,000th home League goal during this season?

346. How much did a match-day programme cost during this season?

347. In January 1978 Watford recorded their biggest win of the season, beating which team 6-0 at home?

348. How many of the club's 46 League games did Watford win?

349. Which manager guided the Hornets to this success?

350. The club recorded the most successive clean sheets at home during this season, but how many - 8, 10 or 12?

# HOW MUCH DID THEY PAY?

*Match up the player with their transfer fee*

| | | |
|---|---|---|
| 351. | John Barnes | £350,000 |
| 352. | Trevor Putney | £2.3 million |
| 353. | Ken Charlery | £8,000 |
| 354. | Bruce Dyer | £900,000 |
| 355. | Mark Falco | £40,000 |
| 356. | Garry Thompson | £3.25 million |
| 357. | Nathan Ellington | £150,000 |
| 358. | Paul Furlong | £12,000 |
| 359. | Barry Dyson | £1.25 million |
| 360. | Ron Wigg | £150,000 |

# NAME THE TEAM

361. Watford played them on the opening day of the Premier League 2006/2007 season.

362. Ray Lewington managed them between 1986 and 1990.

363. Ashley Young scored two goals against them in the Premier League in October 2006.

364. Alhassan Bangura scored his first Watford goal against them in March 2006.

365. Clarke Carlisle signed from this club to join Watford in August 2005.

366. Gavin Mahon made his League debut against them in March 2002.

367. Allan Nielsen signed for Watford from this London side in 2000.

368. Watford beat them to 2nd place by 1 point during 1982/1983 in the Division One table.

369. Watford played their first ever Premier League game against them in August 1999.

370. Jordan Parkes made his debut in the League Cup against them in September 2006?

# TAFFY DAVIES

371. In what year was Taffy born - 1908, 1910 or 1912?

372. How many League games did Taffy play for Watford?

373. Who was the Watford manager when Taffy made his debut for the Hornets?

374. What nationality was Taffy?

375. In what year did Taffy make his debut for the Hornets?

376. What was Taffy's first name - Charles, William or Thomas?

377. In what position did Taffy play for Watford?

378. In which season did Taffy win Player of the Year at Watford?

379. In which year did Taffy play his final game for Watford?

380. How many seasons did Taffy play at Watford - 5, 10 or 20?

# 1980s

381.	How many goals in all competitions did Mark Falco score during 1986/1987, finishing as Watford's top goalscorer?

382.	Who won the Watford Observer Young Player of the Year award in 1982 and 1983?

383.	Who was the Watford manager between May 1987 and January 1988?

384.	Who captained the team in the 1984 FA Cup final?

385.	Paul Wilkinson finished as top League goalscorer during 1988/1989, with how many goals?

386.	In September 1986 which player did Watford sign from Everton for £225,000?

387.	Which player finished as top scorer during 1985/1986 with 13 League and 3 FA Cup goals?

388.	Who was appointed manager of the Hornets in January 1988?

389.	Who won Watford Observer Player of the Year in 1985/1986 and then again in 1986/1987?

390.	During 1981/1982 how much did a Watford match-day programme cost?

# IAN BOLTON

391.  During the championship year of 1977/1978 how many League goals did Ian score - 6, 8 or 10?

392.  From which team did Watford sign Ian in 1977?

393.  How much did Watford pay for Ian?

394.  In which season did Ian win Watford Observer Player of the Year?

395.  How many League games did Ian play for Watford in his career - 134, 234 or 334?

396.  Where was Ian born - Leicester, Leeds or Liverpool?

397.  Who was the only manager that Ian played under whilst at Vicarage Road?

398.  How many League goals did Ian score in his Watford career - 24, 28 or 32?

399.  How many UEFA Cup games did Ian play for Watford in his career?

400.  Which club did Ian sign for when sold for £5,000 in 1983?

# WATFORD V. LUTON TOWN

401.    In April 1983 Watford beat Luton 5-2 at home in
        Division One. Can you name the goalscorers?

402.    In October 1997 Watford beat Luton 4-0 at Kenilworth
        Road. Can you name the three goalscorers?

403.    What was the score when the sides met at Vicarage Road
        in April 1987?

404.    Can you recall the score between the sides when they
        met for the first time in Division One in December 1982?

405.    In April 2006 the sides drew 1-1 in the League. Who
        scored for the Hornets?

406.    Can you name the goalscorers when Watford beat Luton
        Town 2-1 at Kenilworth Road in January 2006?

407.    True or false: the sides have met in the Premier League.

408.    Can you name the season in which the sides first met in
        Division Two?

409.    Which player scored twice against Luton in a 2-2 draw
        in December 1993?

410.    During 1986/1987 Watford beat Luton Town by the
        same scoreline home and away. What was the score in
        both matches?

# LEAGUE CUP SEMI-FINALISTS 2004/2005

411.    Which top-flight team knocked Watford out in the
        semi-finals by beating the Hornets 1-0 in both legs?

412.    Can you name the team that Watford beat 3-0 in the
        quarter-final?

413.    Following on from the previous question, can you name
        the two goalscorers in the game?

414.    Which team did Watford beat 5-2 at Vicarage Road in
        the 4th round?

415.    Following on from the previous question, can you name
        the player who scored twice - including his first goal in
        his Watford career?

416.    Who was the Watford manager in charge of all
        League Cup matches this season?

417.    Can you name the club that Watford beat 1-0 in the
        1st round?

418.    Which team did Watford beat 4-2 away from home on
        penalties in the 3rd round?

419.    Can you name the London team that won the cup final?

420.    Can you name the club that Watford beat 3-0 in the
        2nd round?

# STEWART SCULLION

421. In which year was Stewart born - 1944, 1946 or 1948?

422. How many League games did Stewart play for Watford during his career?

423. How many League goals did Stewart score during his Watford career?

424. Against which team did Stewart score a League brace in a 3-2 win away in September 1968?

425. Against which team did Stewart score a 4th round FA Cup goal in January 1969 in a 1-1 draw?

426. How much did Watford pay for Stewart to join the club club in 1973 for his second spell?

427. Which team did Stewart play for between 1971 and 1973?

428. Which American team did Stewart sign for when leaving Watford in 1976?

429. How many League goals did Stewart score in his 46 League appearances during 1967/1968 - 5, 7 or 9?

430. Can you name the three Watford managers that Stewart played under in his first spell at Vicarage Road?

# RESULTS - 1

*Match up the fixture with the final score*

| | | |
|---|---|---|
| 431. | v. Southampton (Home), September 1980<br>League Cup 2nd Round | 1-4 |
| 432. | v. Shrewsbury Town (Away), October 1961<br>Division Three | 5-1 |
| 433. | v. Machester United (Villa Park), April 2007<br>FA Cup Semi-Final | 5-3 |
| 434. | v. Walsall (Home), April 1989<br>Division Two | 7-1 |
| 435. | v. Notts County (Home), March 1983<br>FA Cup 4th Round | 4-4 |
| 436. | v. West Bromwich Albion (Home), August 1985<br>Division One | 6-1 |
| 437. | v. Tottenham Hotspur (Home), September 1994<br>League Cup 2nd Round, 1st Leg | 1-5 |
| 438. | v. Derby County (Home), January 1982<br>Division Two | 7-2 |
| 439. | v. Everton (Home), February 1984<br>Division One | 5-0 |
| 440. | v. Bradford City (Home), December 1989<br>Division Two | 3-6 |

# DAVID JAMES

441.    In what year was David born - 1966, 1968 or 1970?

442.    David made his Watford League debut in August 1990 in a 2-1 defeat at home to which London club?

443.    Against which country did David make his England debut?

444.    Which Watford manager handed David his Watford debut?

445.    What award did David win in his first season at Vicarage Road?

446.    Following on from the previous question, what was extra special about winning the award?

447.    Which Midlands team did David play for between 1999 and 2001?

448.    David made his England debut in 1997, but in what year did he next play for England for his 2nd cap for his country?

449.    Which manager signed David for Portsmouth in August 2006?

450.    David left Vicarage Road in 1992 and signed for which top-flight team?

# LEAGUE GOALSCORERS - 1

*Match up the player with their highest
League goalscoring achievement*

| | | |
|---|---|---|
| 451. | Tommy Barnett | 65 |
| 452. | Dennis Bond | 68 |
| 453. | Bill Devan | 67 |
| 454. | Roy Brown | 37 |
| 455. | Maurice Cook | 22 |
| 456. | Luther Blissett | 144 |
| 457. | John Barnes | 40 |
| 458. | Harry Lowe | 139 |
| 459. | Fred Pagnam | 33 |
| 460. | Wilf Rostron | 41 |

# 1960s

461. How much was a Watford match-day programme during 1961/1962?

462. In what position did Watford finish in Division 3 in 1966/1967?

463. Which manager was in charge of Watford during 1962/1963?

464. Which player was top goalscorer during 1964/1965 with 19 League goals?

465. Which goalkeeper signed for Watford in 1968 for £5,000 from York City?

466. Which manager took over in 1964 and was manager of Watford until 1971?

467. Who finished as top goalscorer with 12 goals during 1965/1966?

468. Who was Watford manager during 1963/1964?

469. In December 1967 Watford recorded their biggest win of 1967/1968, a 7-1 home win against which team?

470. In what season did Barry Endean score 18 League goals and Tony Garbett 10?

# NIGEL GIBBS

471.    In what position did Nigel play for Watford?

472.    How many League goals did Nigel score for Watford in his career?

473.    In what year was Nigel born - 1955, 1960 or 1965?

474.    Nigel made his Watford League debut in May 1984 at home to which side, with the game ending 0-0?

475.    Against which Midlands team did Nigel score in a 1-0 League away win in August 1988?

476.    Which manager gave Nigel his debut for Watford?

477.    Against which team did Nigel score in both of the home and away 1st and 2nd legs of the League Cup 2nd round, during 1987/1988?

478.    How many UEFA Cup appearances did Nigel make for Watford - 2, 4 or 6?

479.    An injury to which part of his body forced him out of football for over two years in 1992?

480.    Which country did Nigel represent at youth and under-21 level?

# PREMIER LEAGUE 2006/2007

481. Which Watford manager was in charge during this season?

482. Watford recorded their first League win in November 2006, against which side, winning 2-0 at home?

483. Watford won their first point of the season against West Ham United at home, in a 1-1 draw. Can you name the goalscorer?

484. Can you name the two London teams that Watford drew 0-0 with in October 2006?

485. Who scored twice against Fulham in the 3-3 home draw in October 2006?

486. Which goalkeeper did Watford sign on loan from Manchester United in August 2006?

487. Which player left Watford and signed for Aston Villa for £9.65 million in January 2007?

488. What squad number was Tommy Smith given when he signed for Watford in August 2006?

489. Which ex-England international wore squad number 11 during this season?

490. Which two players did Watford sign from Rotherham in January 2007?

# LEAGUE POSITIONS - 1

*Match up the season with Watford's
position in the League*

| 491. | 2005/2006 | 1st |
| --- | --- | --- |
| 492. | 2003/2004 | 23rd |
| 493. | 2001/2002 | 10th |
| 494. | 1999/2000 | 15th |
| 495. | 1997/1998 | 19th |
| 496. | 1995/1996 | 20th |
| 497. | 1993/1994 | 3rd |
| 498. | 1991/1992 | 14th |
| 499. | 1989/1990 | 20th |
| 500. | 1987/1988 | 16th |

# STEVE TERRY

501. In what year was Steve born in London - 1961, 1962 or 1963?

502. Steve made his League debut in April 1980 in a 5-0 defeat, against which side?

503. In what position did Steve play for Watford?

504. How many League appearances did Steve make for Watford - 120, 140 or 160?

505. Which manager gave Steve his debut for the Hornets?

506. How many League goals did Steve score for Watford during his career - 4, 14 or 24?

507. True or False: Steve played in the 1984 FA Cup final.

508. Which team did Steve sign for in March 1990?

509. Steve's father was an international for which country?

510. Steve left Vicarage Road in June 1988 and signed for which team?

# MATCH THE YEAR

*Match up the event with the year it took place*

| | | |
|---|---|---|
| 511. | Watford record their highest home attendance of 34,099 v. Manchester United in the FA Cup | 1986 |
| 512. | Watford participate for the first time in European competition | 2007 |
| 513. | Dave Bassett is appointed as manager | 2005 |
| 514. | Graham Simpson joins the Watford board | 2005 |
| 515. | Watford beats Sockport County 4-1 in the 3rd round of the FA Cup | 1967 |
| 516. | Dixie Hale signs for Watford | 1983 |
| 517. | Aidy Boothroyd is appointed as manager | 1987 |
| 518. | Brian Talbot leaves Vicarage Road and joins Stoke City | 1937 |
| 519. | Marlon King scores his first goal for the Hornets | 1999 |
| 520. | Bill Findlay is appointed as manager | 1969 |

# CLIFF HOLTON

**521.** In what year was Cliff born - 1919, 1929 or 1939?

**522.** How many League goals did Cliff score for Watford during his career - 44, 144 or 244?

**523.** Which manager gave Cliff his Hornets debut?

**524.** In what position did Cliff play for Watford?

**525.** How many goals did Cliff score for Watford during the 1959/1960 season?

**526.** Which London club did Cliff sign from to join Watford?

**527.** Which London club did Cliff play for between 1962 and 1965?

**528.** Which manager signed Cliff in May 1965 for a second spell at the club?

**529.** When Cliff left Watford, which team did he join?

**530.** In what year did Cliff leave Vicarage Road?

# LEAGUE APPEARANCES - 1

*Match up the player with the number of
League appearances he made*

| | | |
|---|---|---|
| 531. | Bill Jannings | 211 |
| 532. | Roger Joslyn | 232 (1) |
| 533. | Dennis Bond | 335 (38) |
| 534. | Luther Blissett | 404 (7) |
| 535. | John Barnes | 80 (13) |
| 536. | Kenny Jackett | 178 (4) |
| 537. | Steve Sherwood | 283 |
| 538. | Paul Wilkinson | 330 (7) |
| 539. | Taffy Davies | 271 (1) |
| 540. | Duncan Welbourne | 135 (1) |

# WATFORD V. ARSENAL

541. In April 1983 Watford beat Arsenal 2-1 at home in Division One. Can you name the goalscorers?

542. In November 1982 Watford beat the Gunners 4-2 at Highbury. Which player scored a brace?

543. Which two players scored when Watford beat Arsenal 2-0 at home in November 1987?

544. What was the score when the sides met for the first time in the Premier League in September 1999?

545. The two sides met in 1999, but in what year during the 1980s did they last meet prior to that?

546. Following on from the previous question, what was the score in the game in 1980s match?

547. True of false: Watford beat Arsenal both home and away in Division One during 1985/1986.

548. Who was the Watford manager when the Hornets beat Arsenal for the first time in a League game?

549. In what year did the sides first ever meet, in the FA Cup, losing 3-0 away?

550. Which two players scored in the 2-0 home League win in March 1987?

# MARLON KING

551. In what year was Marlon born - 1978, 1980 or 1982?

552. Marlon made his Watford debut whilst on loan in August 1995 in a 2-1 defeat to which club?

553. Marlon scored his first Watford goal in only his second game for the club, in a 3-3 draw, against which club?

554. Against which club did Marlon score, and was later sent off, in a 1-1 draw in April 2006?

555. Against which London team did Marlon record his first goal of the 2006/2007 season?

556. For which country has Marlon won international caps?

557. Which Hornets manager brought Marlon to Vicarage Road, initially on loan and then signing him permanently?

558. Which team did Marlon play for between 2000 and 2003?

559. At the start of the 2006/2007 season, which squad number was Marlon given?

560. Which London club did Marlon start at as a trainee and later left the club in 2000?

# POT LUCK - 1

561.  Which ex-Arsenal manager was Watford's first official assistant manager when appointed in 1977?

562.  Who was Watford's assistant manager between 1985 and 1987?

563.  Which newspaper was Watford's main sponsor during 1989/1990?

564.  Who was the club's sponsor during 1983/1984?

565.  During 1991/1992 how much did the most expensive seated match-day ticket cost at Vicarage Road?

566.  Which company was the club's main sponsor during 1988/1989?

567.  Which manager took over from Neil McBain when he left the club in 1959?

568.  Who managed Watford between 1952 and 1955 and then again in 1956?

569.  Watford's worst loss in a game was a 10-0 defeat in 1912, against which Midlands team?

570.  Watford's highest number of wins in a season is 30, but in which season was this record achieved?

# KENNY JACKETT

571.    Kenny was born in Watford in what year - 1958, 1962
        or 1966?

572.    Which country did Kenny represent at youth, under-21
        and full international level?

573.    How many caps did he win at full international level?

574.    How many League goals did Kenny score during his
        career - 15, 25 or 35?

575.    During 1980/1981 how many League goals did Kenny
        score in his 42 appearances?

576.    Kenny made his League debut in April 1980 in a 5-0
        defeat, against which side?

577.    Which Hornets manager gave Kenny his Watford debut?

578.    True or False: Kenny played in the 1984 FA Cup final.

579.    How many UEFA Cup games did Kenny play for Watford
        during his career?

580.    Kenny was appointed as manager of which Welsh team
        in 2004?

# THE FA CUP - 1

581. Can you name the three goalscorers in the 4-1 home win against Stockport County on 6 January 2007?

582. Which player scored 4 goals in the 3rd round 5-0 win in January 1985 against Sheffield United?

583. Who scored a hat-trick against Dagenham in November 1978?

584. Which Essex team did Watford beat 1-0 away during 1980/1981?

585. Which Premier League team did Watford play in the 3rd round in January 2004?

586. In December 1997 Watford played Torquay United in the 2nd round replay, winning 2-1. Which player scored both goals in extra time?

587. Which player scored Watford's goal in the 1-0 4th round win against Swindon Town in January 1995?

588. Which team knocked Watford out of the FA Cup during March 1988 and went on to win the competition?

589. Can you name the club that Watford played in the 1st round during the 1972/1973 season, winning 4-2 at Vicarage Road?

590. Which future manager scored in the 3rd round 2-0 win in January 1990?

# STEVE PERRYMAN

591. In what year was Steve appointed manager of the Hornets?

592. Which manager did Steve take over from at Vicarage Road?

593. Steve brought Paul Furlong to Vicarage Road in 1992, from which club?

594. Steve's first game in charge of Watford was against Barnsley. What was the score?

595. Against which team did Steve record his first win as Watford manager, a 2-0 home win?

596. In what position did Watford finish in Division Two in Steve's first season at Vicarage Road - 10th, 15th or 20th?

597. Which London team did Steve play for between 1969 and 1986?

598. Which team did Steve manage between 1987 and 1990?

599. Which player did Steve buy for Watford in September 1991 from Dagenham?

600. In what year did Steve leave his position as manager of Watford - 1991, 1993 or 1995?

# ROSS JENKINS

**601.** Where was Ross born in 1951?

**602.** From which London club did Watford sign Ross in 1972?

**603.** Which manager signed Ross for Watford?

**604.** In what position did Ross play during his career?

**605.** Which American team did Ross sign for in March 1981 only to return to Watford in September 1981?

**606.** During 1978 Ross and Luther Blissett scored 50 League goals between them. How many goals did Ross score?

**607.** How many League goals did Ross score for Watford during his career - 18, 118 or 218?

**608.** How many League goals did Ross score in his first season at Vicarage Road?

**609.** How many League games in total did Ross play for Watford - 339, 359 or 379?

**610.** Ross won Watford Observer Player of the Year twice during the 1970s, but in which two seasons?

# PLAYER NATIONALITIES - 1

*Match up the player with his nationality*

| | | |
|---|---|---|
| 611. | Marlon King | Nigerian |
| 612. | Tamas Priskin | American |
| 613. | Albert Jarrett | English |
| 614. | Danny Shittu | Estonian |
| 615. | Jay DeMerit | English |
| 616. | Malky Mackay | Jamaican |
| 617. | Tommy Smith | Jamaican |
| 618. | Clarke Carlisle | Sierra Leonean |
| 619. | Damien Francis | Hungarian |
| 620. | Mart Poom | Scottish |

# TONY COTON

621.   In what year was Tony given his Watford debut?

622.   Following on from the previous question, the game finished 5-4 to the opposition, but who were they?

623.   From which Midlands team did Watford sign Tony?

624.   How much did Watford pay for Tony?

625.   Which Hornets manager signed Tony and gave him his Watford debut?

626.   Which team did Tony play for between 1990 and 1996?

627.   In what year was Tony born - 1956, 1961 or 1966?

628.   How many League appearances did Tony make for Watford during his career - 235, 255 or 275?

629.   Which top-flight team did Tony sign for in 1996, but never actually played a League game for them?

630.   In what position did Tony play during his playing days?

# WHERE DID THEY COME FROM? - 1

*Match up the player with the club he was signed from*

| | | |
|---|---|---|
| 631. | Gerry Armstrong | Notts County |
| 632. | Maurice Johnston | Southend United |
| 633. | Brian Talbot | West Bromwich Albion |
| 634. | Peter Kennedy | Leicester City |
| 635. | Tommy Mooney | Tottenham Hotspur |
| 636. | Malky Mackay | Arsenal |
| 637. | Damien Francis | Charlton Athletic |
| 638. | Chris Powell | Partick Thistle |
| 639. | Jordan Stewart | Wigan Athletic |
| 640. | Nathan Ellington | West Ham United |

# PAUL ROBINSON

641.   In which year was Paul born - 1976, 1977 or 1978?

642.   What is Paul's nickname?

643.   Paul made his Watford debut in a 1-1 home draw in October 1996, against which team?

644.   Which Watford manager gave Paul his Hornets debut?

645.   In what position did Paul play for Watford?

646.   Against which London team did Paul score his first Watford goal in October 1997 in a 2-0 home win?

647.   Can you name the team that Paul played his final Watford game against in a 1-0 away win in October 2003?

648.   How many League goals did Paul score for Watford during 2001/2002?

649.   Which Midlands club did Paul sign for after leaving Watford in 2003?

650.   During 2002/2003 Paul scored three League goals for Watford. Can you name two of the three sides he scored against?

# WATFORD V. TOTTENHAM HOTSPUR

651.  In December 1985 Watford beat Spurs 1-0 at home in Division One, but who scored?

652.  What was the score in the Premier League match at Vicarage Road in October 2006?

653.  Which player scored in the first minute of the game in the FA Cup 3rd round match in January 1999?

654.  What was the aggregate score when the sides met in the 1994/1995 League Cup?

655.  Apart from League matches, in which competition did the sides meet during 1986/1987?

656.  Which player, wearing number 8, scored two goals at White Hart Lane in January 1984 in a 3-2 away win?

657.  What was the score when the sides first met in the FA Cup in January 1922 at White Hart Lane?

658.  Who was manager of Watford when the Hornets beat Spurs at Vicarage Road in May 1987?

659.  Which player scored the equaliser in the Premier League home match in March 2000, resulting in a 1-1 draw?

660.  In November 1982 Watford beat Spurs 1-0 at White Hart Lane. Which player, wearing number 4, scored the goal?

# LEAGUE GOALSCORERS - 2

*Match up the player with their highest
League goalscoring achievement*

| | | |
|---|---|---:|
| 661. | Charlie White | 51 |
| 662. | Peter Turner | 28 |
| 663. | Freddie Bunce | 11 |
| 664. | Stewart Scullion | 20 |
| 665. | Charlie Hare | 118 |
| 666. | Ian Bolton | 31 |
| 667. | Ross Jenkins | 81 |
| 668. | Paul Wilkinson | 49 |
| 669. | Dai Ward | 23 |
| 670. | Wally Eames | 34 |

# DUNCAN WELBOURNE

671.   Where was Duncan born in 1940?

672.   In what season did Duncan win Player of the Season at Vicarage Road?

673.   How many League appearances did Duncan make for Watford during his career - 311, 411 or 511?

674.   Which Hornets manager signed Duncan for Watford?

675.   From which team did Watford sign Duncan in 1963?

676.   How many League goals did Duncan score for Watford in his career - 12, 22 or 32?

677.   Duncan scored two League goals during 1970/1971, against which teams?

678.   In which season did Duncan first score a goal for the Hornets?

679.   Duncan scored two League goals during 1971/1972, one against Cardiff City at home, and the other against who?

680.   In what year did Duncan leave Watford to join Southport, later becoming player/coach of the team?

# PLAYER NATIONALITIES - 2

*Match up the player with his nationality*

| | | |
|---|---|---|
| 681. | Hameur Bouazza | French |
| 682. | Gary Porter | Northern Irish |
| 683. | Gavin Mahon | Scottish |
| 684. | Pat Jennings | English |
| 685. | Tom Jones | Jamaican |
| 686. | Toumani Diagouraga | Ivorian |
| 687. | Joe McLaughlin | English |
| 688. | Claude Seanla | English |
| 689. | Joel Grant | Algerian |
| 690. | Kevin Phillips | Welsh |

# PROMOTION TO THE PREMIER LEAGUE - 2005/2006

691. Which team did Watford beat in the play-off final at The Millennium Stadium?

692. Can you name the London team that Watford beat 3-0 on aggregate over the two legs in the semi-final?

693. In what position did Watford finish in the League - 3rd, 4th or 5th?

694. Who was the Watford manager during the promotion year?

695. How many of the 46 League matches did Watford win during the season - 16, 22 or 28?

696. Which Hornets striker finished as top League goalscorer with 21 goals?

697. Can you name the three goalscorers that scored in the 4-1 away win at Sheffield United in February 2006?

698. Which player scored a brace in the 3-1 away win against Southampton in March 2006?

699. Ashley Young scored the only goal to beat which East Anglian side 1-0 in October 2005?

700. Against which team did Watford record their first home win of the season, winning 3-1, with Marlon King and Matthew Spring scoring?

# ROBERT PAGE

701. Which country has Robert represented at international level?

702. Can you name the team that Robert scored his only goal of the 1999/2000 season against?

703. In what position did Robert play for Watford?

704. Robert made his Watford League debut against which Midlands team in October 1993 in a 1-0 defeat?

705. Which manager gave Robert his debut in 1993?

706. In what year was Robert born - 1970, 1974 or 1978?

707. Which Midlands team did Robert sign for in 2005?

708. Against which team did Robert score in a 2-2 away draw in November 1999, with Michael Ngonge scoring the other goal?

709. Can you name the Lancashire team that Robert scored against in April 2001 in a 3-2 away defeat?

710. When Robert left Vicarage Road which team did he sign for?

# DIVISION THREE CHAMPIONS
# - 1968/1969

711.    Who finished as top goalscorer with 18 League goals?

712.    How many of Watford's 46 League games did they win
        - 17, 27 or 37?

713.    Which team finished 2nd, only to lose out to Watford on
        goal difference?

714.    Who was Watford manager during this success?

715.    In January 1969 Watford recorded their biggest League
        win, a 5-0 away win against which team?

716.    Watford were crowned Champions after losing 3-0 to
        which team away from home?

717.    Can you name one of the three players that started in
        all 46 League games?

718.    What was the score when the Hornets played Luton
        Town at home?

719.    Which player scored 5 League goals during the season
        after signing from Luton Town?

720.    How many players were used during the season - 19,
        21 or 23?

# WILF ROSTRON

721. Watford paid which club £150,000 for Wilf in 1979?

722. Wilf won Watford Observer Player of the Season twice, but which two seasons?

723. How many League goals did Wilf score in his first season at Vicarage Road - 3, 6 or 9?

724. Wilf played in six UEFA Cup games for the club during his career, scoring how many goals?

725. In his first season at Watford, against which team did Wilf score in the FA Cup 3rd round?

726. How many League goals did Wilf score for Watford during his Hornets career?

727. Wilf scored his only League goal of the 1986/1987 season in a 5-1 home win against which team?

728. Against which team did Wilf score a brace in September 1985 in a 2-2 away draw?

729. Why didn't Wilf play and captain Watford in the 1984 FA Cup final?

730. Which team did Wilf join when he left Watford in 1989?

# PLAY-OFF WINNERS - 1998/1999

731.   Which team did Watford beat 2-0 in the play-off final?

732.   Which club did Watford beat in the play-off semi-finals, after being 1-1 on aggregate, then beating them 7-6 on penalties?

733.   Which manager led the Hornets to this success?

734.   In what position did Watford finish in the League - 3rd, 4th or 5th?

735.   Which Watford player was top League goalscorer with 10 goals?

736.   Who were the only two players that played in all 46 League matches and the three play-off matches?

737.   Which Watford player scored the only goal in a 1-0 win on the last day of the season against Grimsby Town?

738.   In January 1999 which club did Watford beat 2-1 at Vicarage Road, with Nick Wright and Gifton Noel-Williams scoring - Southampton, Sunderland or Swindon Town?

739.   Which London team did Watford beat 2-1 at home in September 1998, with Keith Millen and Allan Smart scoring?

740.   Watford recorded two 4-1 wins. Can you name the two clubs these games were against?

# RESULTS - 2

*Match up the fixture with the final score*

| 741. | v. Sunderland (Away), April 1972<br>Division Two | 5-2 |
| 742. | v. Barrow (Away), December 1978<br>Division Three | 3-3 |
| 743. | v. Crewe Alexandra (Home), April 1969<br>Division Three | 0-2 |
| 744. | v. Everton (Home), September 1984<br>Division One | 4-1 |
| 745. | v. Crewe Alexandra (Home), October 1977<br>Division Four | 0-5 |
| 746. | v. Doncaster Rovers (Home), March 1977<br>Division Four | 1-6 |
| 747. | v. Bury (Home), January 1979<br>Division Three | 4-3 |
| 748. | v. Blackburn Rovers (Away), December 1992<br>League Cup 4th Round | 4-5 |
| 749. | v. Peterborough United (Away), April 1994<br>Division One | 4-0 |
| 750. | v. Aston Villa (Away), January 2007<br>Premier League | 5-1 |

# GARY PORTER

751.    In what year was Gary born in Sunderland - 1962, 1964 or 1966?

752.    How many League appearances did Gary make for Watford during his career - 296, 396 or 496?

753.    Which Watford manager brought Gary to Watford and handed him his debut?

754.    Against which team did Gary score a League hat-trick in October 1993 in a 4-3 home win?

755.    In March 1987 Gary scored against Arsenal in a 2-0 home win. Which other Hornet scored in the game?

756.    Which country did Gary represent at youth and under-21 level?

757.    How many League goals did Gary score for Watford during his career?

758.    In which season did Gary first score a League goal for Watford?

759.    In what position did Gary play during his playing days?

760.    Gary left Vicarage Road in 1997, signing for which club on a free transfer?

# LEAGUE APPEARANCES - 2

*Match up the player with the number of
League appearances he made*

| | | |
|---|---|---|
| 761. | Stewart Scullion | 94 |
| 762. | Skilly Williams | 97 (3) |
| 763. | Ken Furphy | 100 |
| 764. | Johnny Williams | 304 (8) |
| 765. | David Bardsley | 112 |
| 766. | Pat Rice | 136 |
| 767. | Frank McPherson | 323 |
| 768. | Vic O'Brien | 95 (6) |
| 769. | Arthur Daniels | 371 (3) |
| 770. | Jack Moran | 179 |

# ROGER JOSLYN

771.    Where in Essex was Roger born in 1950?

772.    In what year did Roger make his Watford debut?

773.    Against which team did Roger score a brace in the 3-2 away win in September 1978?

774.    How many League appearances did Roger make for Watford - 102, 182 or 262?

775.    During 1975/1976 Roger scored three League goals for Watford, against which three teams?

776.    How many League goals did Roger score in his Watford career?

777.    How many League goals did Roger score in his first season at Vicarage Road?

778.    Against which team did Roger score a brace in a 6-0 win in January 1978?

779.    Which manager brought Roger to Watford?

780.    Which club did Roger sign for when he left Watford in 1979 for £40,000?

# TOMMY MOONEY

781.    From which Essex side did Watford sign Tommy?

782.    In which year did Tommy sign for Watford - 1992, 1993 or 1994?

783.    Against which team did Tommy make his Watford League debut in a 2-0 defeat?

784.    In what year was Tommy born - 1970, 1971 or 1972?

785.    How many goals did Tommy score during 2000/2001, in all competitions?

786.    Against which team did Tommy score the only goal in a 1-0 Premier League away win in August 1999?

787.    Against which Essex based team did Tommy score a brace in a 3-0 home win in August 2001?

788.    Against which team did Tommy score a hat-trick at home in a 4-0 win in December 2001?

789.    How many League goals did Tommy score during 1997/1998 - 2, 6 or 10?

790.    Tommy left Vicarage Road in 2001. Which Midlands side did he sign for?

# POT LUCK - 2

791.  Can you name the chairman who brought out Elton John in 1990?

792.  Who won Watford Player of the Season in 1959/1960 and then again in 1960/1961?

793.  Who's testimonial match was against Arsenal in April 1969?

794.  Who was the club's official sponsor during 1993/1994?

795.  Can you name the 'Road' Watford played at before moving to Vicarage Road in 1922?

796.  Which Rugby club plays at Vicarage Road and has used it as their home ground since 1997?

797.  Can you name Watford's two honorary presidents?

798.  'The Hornets' is the name that most fans associate with Watford, but can you recall their other nickname?

799.  Which ex-Spurs manager was appointed assistant manager in March 2005?

800.  Can you name the year in which Watford played their first Premier League game?

# ALEC CHAMBERLAIN

801. In what position did Alec play?

802. For which team did Alec play between 1988 and 1993 - Chelsea, Wimbledon or Luton Town?

803. In 2005 Alec was awarded his testimonial whilst playing for Watford. Against which top-flight team did Watford lose this match 2-1 - Charlton Athletic, West Ham United or Crystal Palace?

804. In what year was Alec born - 1960, 1962 or 1964?

805. Which manager signed Alec for Watford in 1996?

806. Against which team did Alec make his Watford debut in August 1996 in a 2-0 away win?

807. From which team did Watford sign Alec?

808. What squad number was Alec given at the start of the 2006/2007 season - 1, 13 or 27?

809. How many League appearances did Alec make in his first season at Watford - 4, 14 or 24?

810. Which Essex side did Alec play for between 1982 and 1987?

# WHERE DID THEY GO? - 2

*Match up the player with the club they joined after leaving Watford*

| | | |
|---|---|---|
| 811. | John Barnes | Walsall |
| 812. | Gifton Noel-Williams | Herfolge |
| 813. | Michel Ngonge | Reading |
| 814. | Darren Bazeley | Brentford |
| 815. | Allan Nielsen | Stoke City |
| 816. | Robert Page | Queens Park Rangers |
| 817. | Neal Ardley | Bristol City |
| 818. | Marcus Gayle | Sheffield United |
| 819. | Brynjar Gunnarsson | Cardiff City |
| 820. | Keith Millen | Liverpool |

# GIANLUCA VIALLI

821.    In what year was Gianluca appointed Hornets manager?

822.    Which Watford manager did Gianluca take over from?

823.    Can you name the London side that Gianluca managed between 1998 and 2000?

824.    Gianluca's first League game in charge of Watford was against which side, losing 3-0 away?

825.    To what position in the League did Gianluca guide Watford in his only season in charge - 4th, 14th or 24th?

826.    Can you name the three Italian teams Gianluca played for during his career?

827.    Against which team did Watford record their first League win with Gianluca in charge, a 3-2 home win in August 2001, with Tommy Smith (2) and Allan Neilsen scoring?

828.    What nationality is Gianluca?

829.    How many international caps did Gianluca win for his country, having scored 16 goals?

830.    Which manager took over at Vicarage Road when Gianluca left in 2002?

# COMINGS AND GOINGS - 1

831. Which 'James' signed for Cardiff City on loan from Vicarage Road in November 2006?

832. Which Jamaican international forward did Watford sign from Rangers in 2001?

833. When Neil Redfearn left Vicarage Road in 1990, which club did he sign for, costing them £150,000?

834. Which 'Willie' signed for the Hornets from Aberdeen in June 1988?

835. Which former Gunner signed for Watford on loan during 1991, making 8 League appearances for the club?

836. When Tim Sherwood left Vicarage Road in July 1989, which East Anglian team did he join?

837. Which 'Roger' signed for Watford in October 1992 from Barnet and then signed for Birmingham City in 1993?

838. Which forward signed for Rangers on leaving Vicarage Road in May 1986?

839. Which Swiss international defender signed for Watford in 2001 on a free transfer from Celtic?

840. Which Midlands team signed Paul Devlin on leaving Watford in January 2006?

# AIDY BOOTHROYD

841. In which year was Aidy appointed as Watford manager?

842. Which Scottish team did Aidy play for between 1992 and 1993?

843. Which position did Aidy play during his playing days?

844. What nationality is Aidy - Welsh, Scottish or English?

845. At what age did Aidy retire from playing football due to injury?

846. Which team was Aidy playing for when he retired from football in 1998?

847. In 2006, what was the first honour that Aidy as manager helped Watford to achieve?

848. At which club was Aidy appointed first-team coach in the summer of 2004?

849. Which manager did Aidy take over from at Vicarage Road when he was appointed?

850. In what year was Aidy born - 1969, 1971 or 1973?

# DIVISION TWO CHAMPIONS
# - 1997/1998

851.    Which Hornets manager led Watford to this success?

852.    Which Watford player finished as the highest League
        goalscorer with eleven goals?

853.    Watford finished as Champions, but which other two
        sides got promoted with them?

854.    In October 1997, Watford beat Luton Town 4-0 away.
        Can you name the three goalscorers (one player scoring
        two goals)?

855.    Which London side did Watford beat 2-1 on the last day
        of the season to seal promotion in May 1998?

856.    Following on from the previous question, can you name
        the two goalscorers?

857.    Which former Liverpool and Tottenham forward scored
        eight League goals for the Hornets during this season?

858.    In November 1997 Peter Kennedy scored a hat-trick
        in a 3-0 away win against which Essex side?

859.    Which team did Watford beat 1-0 on the opening day of
        the season, with Jason Lee scoring on his debut?

860.    How many points did Watford finish with - 88, 98 or
        108?

# BIG WINS - 2

*Match up Watford's winning score with
the match in which it was achieved*

861. **v. West Bromwich Albion (Home)**
     **Division 1, August 1985**                          **4-0**

862. **v. Chelsea (Away)**
     **Division 1, May 1986**                             **4-0**

863. **v. Sheffield United (Home)**
     **FA Cup 3rd Round, January 1985**                   **4-1**

864. **v. Wolverhampton Wanderers (Away)**
     **Division 1, December 1983**                        **5-1**

865. **v. Sunderland (Home)**
     **Division 1, September 1982**                       **5-0**

866. **v. Brighton & Hove Albion (Home)**
     **Division 1, November 1982**                        **5-1**

867. **v. Tranmere Rovers (Home)**
     **Division 3, September 1978**                        **5-1**

868. **v. Southport (Home)**
     **Division 3, March 1974**                           **5-0**

869. **v. Scunthorpe United (Home)**
     **Division 3, March 1973**                           **4-0**

870. **v. Portsmouth (Home)**
     **Division 2, October 1969**                         **8-0**

# WATFORD V. WEST HAM UNITED

871.    In December 1982 Watford beat West Ham 2-1 at
        Vicarage Road. Which players scored the goals?

872.    What was the score when the sides met at Vicarage Road
        in the Premier League in August 2006?

873.    The sides met in the FA Cup 4th round in January 1982,
        Watford winning 2-0. Which two players scored the
        goals?

874.    What was the score when the sides met in Febraury 1984
        at Upton Park with John Barnes scoring twice in the
        game?

875.    What was the score when the sides met for the first
        time in the Premier League in September 1999 at
        Upton Park?

876.    What was the score when the sides met in the League
        in April 1985?

877.    True of false: West Ham beat Watford both home and
        away in Division One in 1985/1986.

878.    In September 1979 which striker scored both goals in a
        2-0 home win?

879.    In what year did the sides first meet in Division One?

880.    Following on from the previous question, what was the
        score at Vicarage Road?

# NIGEL CALLAGHAN

881. In what year was Nigel born - 1960, 1962 or 1964?

882. Nigel made his Watford League debut in September 1980 in a 2-1 home win, against which team?

883. In what country was Nigel born?

884. Nigel made six UEFA Cup appearances for Watford during his career, scoring how many goals?

885. Against which team did Nigel score a brace in a 4-0 away win in October 1984 in the League Cup?

886. During 1985/1986 Nigel scored four League goals. Can you name the teams he scored against?

887. Which country did Nigel represent at under-21 and 'B' level?

888. How many League goals did Nigel score for Watford during his Watford career?

889. In August 1982 Nigel scored a brace against which team in a 4-1 away League win?

890. In February 1987 Nigel left Vicarage Road and signed for which team?

# DIVISION THREE RUNNERS-UP
# - 1978/1979

891. Which team did Watford finish one point behind to become runners-up of Division Three?

892. How many League goals did Watford score this season - 63, 73 or 83?

893. Which team did Watford beat 4-0 on the final day of the season?

894. Can you name the only two players that started every League match?

895. Who was the Hornets manager?

896. Can you name the team that Watford recorded their biggest League win of the season against, a 5-0 away win in September 1978?

897. How many League goals did Luther Blissett score during the season?

898. Which Hornet was top goalscorer with 29 League goals?

899. How much did a Watford match-day programme cost during this season?

900. How many of the 46 League matches did Watford win - 14, 24 or 34?

# FA CUP SEMI-FINALISTS - 1987

901.    Which London team sadly knocked Watford out in the semi-final?

902.    Can you name the London team that Watford knocked out in the quarter-finals?

903.    Following on from the previous question, can you recall the score?

904.    Can you name the player who scored twice in the quarter-final?

905.    Watford beat Maidstone 3-1 in the 3rd round at Vicarage Road. Which player scored a brace in the game?

906.    Which goalkeeper started the semi-final for Watford, this being his only appearance of the season for the club?

907.    Which player scored four FA Cup goals during Watford's run?

908.    Which London club did Watford beat 1-0 in the 4th round at Vicarage Road?

909.    Following on from the previous question, which player scored the goal?

910.    Which Midlands team did Watford play in the 5th round and two replays, beating them in the second replay 1-0 away?

# HOW MUCH DID I COST?

*Match up the player with their transfer fee*

| | | |
|---|---|---|
| 911. | Gerry Armstrong | Free Transfer |
| 912. | Pat Jennings | £150,000 |
| 913. | Steve Sherwood | £250,000 |
| 914. | Tony Coton | £1,300 |
| 915. | Lee Nogan | £6,000 |
| 916. | John McClelland | £100,000 |
| 917. | Perry Suckling | £300,000 |
| 918. | Brian Talbot | £3,000 |
| 919. | Duncan Welbourne | £300,000 |
| 920. | Devon White | £225,000 |

# FA CUP FINAL - 1984

921.  Who did Watford play in the FA Cup final?

922.  Which Watford manager led the Hornets to the Cup final?

923.  Can you recall the score in the game?

924.  Following on from the previous question, can you name the goalscorers?

925.  Can you name seven of the starting eleven for Watford?

926.  Which team did Watford beat in the semi-final of the FA Cup?

927.  Which London club did Watford beat 2-0 in the 4th round?

928.  At which stadium was the game played?

929.  Can you name the team that Watford beat in the 3rd round? The score in the game was 2-2 and they beat the opposition 4-3 in the replay.

930.  Which Midlands team did Watford knock out in the quarter-finals?

# LEAGUE POSITIONS - 2

*Match up the season with Watford's position in the League*

| | | |
|---|---|---|
| 931. | 1985/1986 | 18th |
| 932. | 1983/1984 | 8th |
| 933. | 1981/1982 | 19th |
| 934. | 1979/1980 | 7th |
| 935. | 1977/1978 | 6th |
| 936. | 1975/1976 | 1st |
| 937. | 1973/1974 | 12th |
| 938. | 1971/1972 | 2nd |
| 939. | 1969/1970 | 22nd |
| 940. | 1967/1968 | 11th |

# DIVISION ONE RUNNERS-UP
# - 1982/1983

941. To whom did Watford finish runners-up, eleven points behind them?

942. How many of the 42 League games did the Hornets win - 20, 22 or 24?

943. Which team did Watford beat 8-0 at Vicarage Road in September 1982?

944. Can you name any of the three players that started in every League game?

945. Which player, wearing number 9, scored a brace against Manchester City at home in January 1983?

946. Can you name the only month during the season that Watford won all their League matches?

947. Which player, wearing number 8, scored in the first two League games against Everton and Southampton?

948. Who was the Watford chairman during this season?

949. Which Hampshire based team did Watford beat both home (2-0) and away (4-1)?

950. Which Hornet finished as top goalscorer with 27 League goals?

# COMINGS AND GOINGS - 2

951. Which ex-England international signed for the Hornets from Reading in September 2005?

952. Who signed from Bolton Wanderers for £500,000 in November 1999?

953. Watford signed Kerry Dixon in 1996 from Millwall, but he left in the same year, signing for which club?

954. Which French midfielder signed for Le Havre in 2000 after leaving Watford?

955. Which West Ham United player spent a month on loan at Vicarage Road during September-October 2005, making three appearances for the club?

956. Which 'Bruce' signed for Stoke City when leaving Vicarage Road in August 2005?

957. In December 2002 which Norwegian international goalkeeper signed for Everton on leaving Watford?

958. Which team did Jason Lee sign for when he left Watford in 1998?

959. Which Yorkshire based team did Lee Sinnott sign for on leaving Vicarage Road in July 1987?

960. Which Welsh international goalkeeper spent two months on loan to Watford between December 2004 and February 2005, making nine League appearances?

# JOHN McCLELLAND

961. In what year was John born - 1953, 1954 or 1955?

962. Which country did John represent and captain at full international level?

963. In what year did John join Watford?

964. From which Scottish club did Watford sign John?

965. During 1986/1987 John scored his only League goal of the season in a 2-0 home win, against which side?

966. How many League goals did John score for Watford in his 187 appearances for the club?

967. Which Yorkshire team did John sign for in June 1989 only to return to Watford in January 1990 on loan?

968. How many full international caps did John win - 13, 53 or 93?

969. Against which team did John score in March 1985, his only goal of the 1984/1985 season?

970. In what position did John play for Watford?

# WHERE DID THEY COME FROM? - 2

*Match up the player with the club he was signed from*

| | | |
|---|---|---|
| 971. | Darius Henderson | Nottingham Forest |
| 972. | Bruce Dyer | Arsenal |
| 973. | Neil Cox | Coventry City |
| 974. | Johann Gudmundsson | Bolton Wanderers |
| 975. | Jason Lee | Tottenham Hotspur |
| 976. | Steve Palmer | Gillingham |
| 977. | Ronny Rosenthal | IB Keflavik |
| 978. | Pat Rice | Derby County |
| 979. | Tommy Smith | Ipswich Town |
| 980. | Paul Furlong | Barnsley |

# HEIDAR HELGUSON

981. In which country was Heidar born?

982. Which Watford manager signed Heidar for the club in 2000?

983. Heidar scored on his Hornets debut in a 3-2 home defeat, against which side?

984. How many goals did Heidar score in his first season at Watford duing 1999/2000 - 5, 6 or 7?

985. Following on from the previous question, can you name three of the teams Heidar scored against?

986. From which club did Watford sign Heidar?

987. Against which Yorkshire team did Heidar score a brace in a 3-0 win, with Tommy Smith scoring the other, during
    November 2001?

988. In May 2005 Heidar made his final appearance for Waford, scoring in a 2-1 defeat, against which side?

989. During Heidar's last season (2004/2005) at Watford, how many goals did he score for them (including League Cup and FA Cup goals) - 15, 20 or 25?

990. When Heidar left Vicarage Road which London Premier League team did he sign for?

# POT LUCK - 3

991. In what year did Graham Simpson become Executive Chairman of Watford and Watford Leisure PLC?

992. Which player was top League goalscorer with 22 League goals during 1976/1977?

993. Which 'David' won Player of the Year during 1961/1962?

994. How many League appearances did Frank Smith make for the Hornets - 219, 319 or 419?

995. Who was appointed as the club's assistant manager in 1991?

996. Which player got sent off twice during 1976/1977, once against Bournemouth (away) and again against Huddersfield Town (home)?

997. What is the club's postal code at Vicarage Road?

998. During 1962/1963 which player finished top League goalscorer with 29 goals?

999. Which player was handed the number 33 squad number during 2006/2007?

1000. What was the first year in their history that Watford played a Division One match?

# ANSWERS

## THE CLUB - RECORDS & HISTORY
1.  The Hornets
2.  1881
3.  Tottenham Hotspur
4.  1920
5.  Cliff Holton
6.  Luther Blissett
7.  Manchester United
8.  John Barnes
9.  8-0 to Watford
10. 1922

## LUTHER BLISSETT
11. 1958
12. Luxembourg
13. 158
14. 3
15. AC Milan
16. Barnsley
17. Score for England
18. Mike Keen
19. 14
20. Centre forward

## MANAGERS
| | | |
|---|---|---|
| 21. | Ray Lewington | 2002-2005 |
| 22. | Glenn Roeder | 1993-1996 |
| 23. | Mike Keen | 1973-1977 |
| 24. | Len Goulden | 1952-1955 |
| 25. | Steve Perryman | 1990-1993 |
| 26. | Graham Taylor | 1996-2001 |
| 27. | Eddie Hapgood | 1948-1950 |
| 28. | Graham Taylor | 1977-1987 |
| 29. | Neil McBain | 1929-1937 |
| 30. | Gianluca Vialli | 2001-2002 |

## GRAHAM TAYLOR
31. Lincoln City
32. 1977
33. Hungary
34. OBE
35. "Do I Not Like That?"

36. Wolverhampton Wanderers
37. Grimsby Town
38. 38
39. Gianluca Vialli
40. 1944

## WHERE DID THEY GO? - 1

| 41. | Andy Hessenthaler | Gillingham |
| --- | --- | --- |
| 42. | Hameur Bouazza | Fulham |
| 43. | Neil Redfearn | Oldham Athletic |
| 44. | David Connolly | Feyenoord |
| 45. | Matthew Spring | Luton Town |
| 46. | Clint Easton | Norwich City |
| 47. | Paul Devlin | Walsall |
| 48. | Neil Cox | Cardiff City |
| 49. | Paul Robinson | West Bromwich Albion |
| 50. | Gary Penrice | Bristrol Rovers |

## STEVE SHERWOOD

51. 1953
52. Goalkeeper
53. 1
54. 1977
55. 211
56. 6 - all of them
57. Graham Taylor
58. He was an Olympic Bronze hurdler
59. Grimsby Town
60. Hearts

## PLAYER OF THE YEAR - 1

| 61. | 1972/1973 | Andy Rankin |
| --- | --- | --- |
| 62. | 1974/1975 | Andy Rankin |
| 63. | 1976/1977 | Keith Mercer |
| 64. | 1978/1979 | Ross Jenkins |
| 65. | 1980/1981 | Steve Sims |
| 66. | 1982/1983 | Wilf Rostron |
| 67. | 1984/1985 | John McClelland |
| 68. | 1986/1987 | Tony Coton |
| 69. | 1988/1989 | Glyn Hodges |
| 70. | 1990/1991 | David James |

## PREMIER LEAGUE - 1999/2000

71. Liverpool
72. Heidar Helguson
73. 6
74. Graham Taylor
75. Allan Smart
76. Sheffield Wednesday
77. David Perpetuini and Xavier Gravelaine (2)
78. Steve Palmer
79. Heidar Helguson
80. Tommy Mooney

## MATCH OF THE YEAR - 1

| 81. | FA Cup Runners-Up | 1984 |
|---|---|---|
| 82. | League Cup Semi-Finalists | 1979 |
| 83. | Division Three Champions | 1969 |
| 84. | League Cup Semi-Finalists | 2004 |
| 85. | FA Cup Semi-Finalists | 2003 |
| 86. | Division Four Champions | 1978 |
| 87. | Division One Runners-Up | 1983 |
| 88. | Division Two Champions | 1998 |
| 89. | Championship Play-off Winners | 2006 |
| 90. | First Division Play-off Winners | 1999 |

## DARREN WARD

91. 1978
92. Luton Town
93. 3
94. Middlesbrough
95. Defender (Central)
96. Cheltenham Town
97. Paolo Vernazza and Tommy Smith
98. Crystal Palace
99. Queens Park Rangers
100. Millwall

## TOP LEAGUE GOALSCORERS IN A SEASON

| 101. | 1996/1997 | Tommy Mooney | 13 |
|---|---|---|---|
| 102. | 1997/1998 | Peter Kennedy | 11 |
| 103. | 1998/1999 | Gifton Noel-Williams | 10 |
| 104. | 1999/2000 | Heidar Helguson | 6 |
| 105. | 2000/2001 | Tommy Mooney | 19 |

| 106. | 2001/2002 | Tommy Smith | 11 |
| 107. | 2002/2003 | Heidar Helguson | 11 |
| 108. | 2003/2004 | Scott Fitzgerald | 10 |
| 109. | 2004/2005 | Heidar Helguson | 16 |
| 110. | 2005/2006 | Marlon King | 21 |

## THE UEFA CUP - 1983/1984

111. Jimmy Gilligan
112. Graham Taylor
113. Steve Sims
114. 10
115. Kevin Richardson
116. Steve Sherwood, Charlie Palmer, Kenny Jackett, Richard Jobson, Steve Sims, Paul Franklin, Nigel Callaghan, John Barnes, Jimmy Gilligan, Jan Lohman and Wilf Rostron
117. John Barnes, Nigel Callaghan, Wilf Rostron and Steve Sherwood
118. Kaiserslautern
119. Jimmy Gilligan
120. Sparta Prague

## WHO AM I?

121. David James
122. John Barnes
123. Alec Chamberlain
124. Maurice Johnston
125. Graham Taylor
126. Nigel Gibbs
127. Damien Francis
128. Brian Talbot
129. Luther Blissett
130. Nigel Callaghan

## PROMOTION TO DIVISION ONE - 1981/1982

131. 23
132. 2nd
133. Graham Taylor
134. Les Taylor and Ian Bolton
135. Luther Blissett
136. Derby County
137. 76
138. Queens Park Rangers
139. John Barnes and Ross Jenkins

140. 2

## TOM WALLEY
141. 1945
142. Ken Furphy
143. Midfielder
144. 1
145. Wales
146. 217: 214 (3)
147. Arsenal
148. First team coach
149. 17
150. Player of the Season

## PAT JENNINGS
151. 1945
152. 52
153. £6,000
154. Bill McGarry
155. Wales (April 1964)
156. MBE
157. Arsenal
158. Goalkeeper
159. Northern Ireland
160. Tottenham Hotspur

## HAT-TRICK HEROES
161. v. Port Vale (Home)
Apr 1996, League, 5-2 win      David Connolly
162. v. Grimsby Town (Home)
Apr 1996, League, 6-3 win      David Connolly
163. v. Grimsby Town (Home)
Apr 1996, League, 6-3 win      Craig Ramage
164. v. Norwich City (Home)
Dec 2001, League, 4-0 win      Tommy Mooney
165. v. Southend United (Away)
Feb 1995, League, 4-0 win      Darren Bazeley
166. v. Bolton Wanderers (Home)
Oct 1993, League, 4-3 win      Gary Porter
167. v. Blackpool (Home)
Aug 1978, League, 5-1 win      Ross Jenkins

| 168. | v. Dagenham (Home) | |
|---|---|---|
| | Nov 1978, FA Cup 1st Round, 3-0 win | Ross Jenkins |
| 169. | v. Wolves (Away) | |
| | Dec 1983, League, 5-0 win | Maurice Johnston |
| 170. | v. Notts County (Home) | |
| | Mar 1983, FA Cup 6th round, 5-3 win | Luther Blissett |

## DAMIEN FRANCIS

171. 1979
172. 7
173. Aidy Boothroyd
174. Everton
175. Norwich City
176. £1.5 million
177. Wimbledon/Milton Keynes Dons
178. Newcastle United
179. Manchester United
180. Jamaican

## MAURICE JOHNSTON

181. Manchester United
182. Glasgow
183. 20
184. Nantes
185. 14
186. 23
187. Partick Thistle
188. Graham Taylor
189. Everton
190. Celtic

## STEVE PALMER

191. 1968
192. Ipswich Town
193. Defender (Central)
194. Tranmere Rovers
195. Crewe Alexandra (Away) and Preston North End (Home)
196. Norwich City
197. Milton Keynes Dons
198. 8
199. Preston North End
200. Queens Park Rangers

**1990s**

201.   4-0 to Watford
202.   Kevin Phillips
203.   Jason Lee
204.   Blackpool
205.   Liverpool
206.   Steve Harrison, Colin Lee and Steve Perryman
207.   Darren Bazeley
208.   Andy Hessenthaler and Tommy Mooney
209.   Paul Furlong
210.   David Perpetuini and Xavier Gravelaine

**ANDY RANKIN**

211.   1944
212.   Everton
213.   £12,500
214.   19
215.   George Kirby
216.   Huddersfield Town
217.   George Kirby, Mike Keen and Graham Taylor
218.   England
219.   Skilly Williams
220.   299

**BIG WINS - 1**

221.   v. Stockport County (Home)
       FA Cup 3rd Round, January 2007          4-1
222.   v. Southampton (Home)
       League Cup 4th Round, November 2004     5-2
223.   v. Coventry City (Home)
       League, August 2002                     5-2
224.   v. Grimsby Town (Home)
       League, November 2000                   4-0
225.   v. Blackpool (Home)
       League, November 1997                   4-1
226.   v. Grimsby Town (Home)
       League, April 1996                      6-3
227.   v. Southend United (Away)
       League, February 1995                   4-0
228.   v. Bristol City (Home)
       League, May 1992                        5-2

| 229. | v. Bradford City (Home) | |
| | League, December 1989 | 7-2 |
| 230. | v. Darlington (Home) | |
| | League Cup 2nd Round, October 1987 | 8-0 |

## WATFORD V. CHELSEA
231.   1-0 to Watford
232.   Allan Smart
233.   1-0 to Watford
234.   Malcom Poskett
235.   David Bardsley, Luther Blissett and Gary Porter
236.   Luther Blissett
237.   Heidar Helguson and Gavin Mahon
238.   5-1 to Watford
239.   True
240.   Steve Terry, Luther Blissett and John Barnes

## FA CUP SEMI-FINALISTS 2003
241.   Macclesfield Town
242.   Heidar Helguson and Jermaine Pennant
243.   Sunderland
244.   2-0
245.   Tommy Smith and Stephen Glass
246.   Southampton
247.   2-1 to Southampton
248.   Marcus Gayle
249.   Villa Park
250.   Heidar Helguson

## THE LEAGUE CUP
251.   Lee Logan
252.   Accrington Stanley
253.   1-0 to Middlesbrough
254.   Wolverhampton Wanderers
255.   Scott Fitzgerald
256.   Hull City
257.   Tommy Smith, Darren Ward and Heidar Helguson
258.   2-0 to Watford
259.   Southend United
260.   Danny Shittu and Damien Francis

## JOHN BARNES

261.     Jamaica
262.     1981
263.     Oldham Athletic
264.     10
265.     Newcastle United
266.     65
267.     Celtic
268.     Liverpool
269.     10
270.     11

## LES TAYLOR

271.     Midfield
272.     Oxford United
273.     4
274.     He was the Watford captain
275.     Luton Town
276.     13
277.     Graham Taylor
278.     1956
279.     172: 167 (5)
280.     Reading

## 1970s

281.     Ross Jenkins
282.     Steve Sims
283.     Keith Mercer
284.     Colin Franks
285.     Keith Eddy
286.     7th
287.     Andy Rankin
288.     37 goals: 29 League, 4 FA Cup, 4 League Cup
289.     5 pence
290.     Mike Keen

## STEVE SIMS

291.     Leicester City
292.     Graham Taylor
293.     Colchester United
294.     Aston Villa
295.     171

| | | |
|---|---|---|
| 296. | *£175,000* | |
| 297. | *5* | |
| 298. | *1* | |
| 299. | *England* | |
| 300. | *Notts County* | |

## PAT RICE

| | | |
|---|---|---|
| 301. | *1980* | |
| 302. | *1* | |
| 303. | *Northern Irish* | |
| 304. | *Defender (Right Back)* | |
| 305. | *Arsenal* | |
| 306. | *112* | |
| 307. | *Graham Taylor* | |
| 308. | *Arsenal youth team coach* | |
| 309. | *49* | |
| 310. | *1949* | |

## GLENN ROEDER

| | | |
|---|---|---|
| 311. | *1996* | |
| 312. | *Leyton Orient* | |
| 313. | *1989* | |
| 314. | *1955* | |
| 315. | *West Ham United* | |
| 316. | *1* | |
| 317. | *Gillingham* | |
| 318. | *Queens Park Rangers and Newcastle United* | |
| 319. | *39* | |
| 320. | *Newcastle United* | |

## SQUAD NUMBERS - 2007/2008

| | | |
|---|---|---|
| 321. | *Lloyd Doyley* | *12* |
| 322. | *Damien Francis* | *7* |
| 323. | *Lee Williamson* | *14* |
| 324. | *Jobi McAnuff* | *11* |
| 325. | *Gareth Williams* | *25* |
| 326. | *Gavin Mahon* | *8* |
| 327. | *Mart Poom* | *1* |
| 328. | *Nathan Ellington* | *18* |
| 329. | *Tommy Smith* | *21* |
| 330. | *John O'Toole* | *35* |

## CAPS FOR MY COUNTRY

| | | |
|---|---|---|
| 331. | Chris Powell | 5 England Caps |
| 332. | John Barnes | 79 England Caps |
| 333. | Kenny Jackett | 31 Wales Caps |
| 334. | Tony Coton | 1 England B Cap |
| 335. | Luther Blissett | 14 England Caps |
| 336. | Mark Watson | 77 Canada Caps |
| 337. | Iwan Roberts | 15 Wales Caps |
| 338. | David Bardsley | 2 England Caps |
| 339. | Gerry Armstrong | 63 Northern Ireland Caps |
| 340. | Pat Jennings | 119 Northern Ireland Caps |

## DIVISION FOUR CHAMPIONS - 1977/1978

| | |
|---|---|
| 341. | Southend United |
| 342. | Alan Garner |
| 343. | 16 |
| 344. | 23 |
| 345. | Alan Garner |
| 346. | 15 pence |
| 347. | Doncaster Rovers |
| 348. | 30 (18 home and 12 away) |
| 349. | Graham Taylor |
| 350. | 10 |

## HOW MUCH DID THEY PAY?

| | | |
|---|---|---|
| 351. | John Barnes | £900,000 |
| 352. | Trevor Putney | £40,000 |
| 353. | Ken Charlery | £150,000 |
| 354. | Bruce Dyer | £1.25 million |
| 355. | Mark Falco | £350,000 |
| 356. | Garry Thompson | £150,000 |
| 357. | Nathan Ellington | £3.25 million |
| 358. | Paul Furlong | £2.3 million |
| 359. | Barry Dyson | £8,000 |
| 360. | Ron Wigg | £12,000 |

## NAME THE TEAM

| | |
|---|---|
| 361. | Everton |
| 362. | Fulham |
| 363. | Fulham |
| 364. | Derby County |
| 365. | Leeds United |

366. *Crystal Palace*
367. *Tottenham Hotspur*
368. *Manchester United*
369. *Wimbledon (Milton Keynes Dons)*
370. *Accrington Stanley*

## TAFFY DAVIES
371. *1910*
372. *283*
373. *Neil McBain*
374. *Welsh*
375. *1931*
376. *William*
377. *Winger/Inside Forward*
378. *1947/1948*
379. *1950*
380. *20*

## 1980s
381. *16: 14 League, 2 FA Cup*
382. *John Barnes*
383. *Dave Bassett*
384. *Les Taylor*
385. *18*
386. *Kevin Richardson*
387. *Colin West*
388. *Steve Harrison*
389. *Tony Coton*
390. *30 pence*

## IAN BOLTON
391. *6*
392. *Lincoln City*
393. *£12,000*
394. *1979/1980*
395. *234: 233 (1)*
396. *Leicester*
397. *Graham Taylor*
398. *28*
399. *3*
400. *Brentford*

## WATFORD V. LUTON TOWN
401.   Nigel Callaghan, Luther Blissett (2), John Barnes and Richard
       Jobson
402.   Richard Johnson, Dai Thomas and Peter Kennedy (2)
403.   2-0 to Watford
404.   1-0 to Luton Town
405.   Marlon King
406.   Darius Henderson and Malky Mackay
407.   False
408.   1970/1971
409.   Bruce Dyer
410.   2-0 to Watford

## LEAGUE CUP SEMI-FINALISTS 2004/2005
411.   Liverpool
412.   Portsmouth
413.   Heidar Helguson (2) and Bruce Dyer
414.   Southampton
415.   James Chambers
416.   Ray Lewington
417.   Cambridge United
418.   Sheffield United
419.   Chelsea
420.   Reading

## STEWART SCULLION
421.   1946
422.   312
423.   49
424.   Crewe Alexandra
425.   Manchester United
426.   £15,000
427.   Sheffield United
428.   Tampa Bay Rowdies
429.   9
430.   Ken Furphy, George Kirby and Mike Keen

## RESULTS - 1
431.   v. Southampton (Home), September 1980
       League Cup 2nd Round                              7-1
432.   v. Shrewsbury Town (Away), October 1961
       Division Three                                    1-5

| 433. | v. Machester United (Villa Park), April 2007 | |
| | FA Cup Semi-Final | 1-4 |
| 434. | v. Walsall (Home), April 1989 | |
| | Division Two | 5-0 |
| 435. | v. Notts County (Home), March 1983 | |
| | FA Cup 4th Round | 5-3 |
| 436. | v. West Bromwich Albion (Home), August 1985 | |
| | Division One | 5-1 |
| 437. | v. Tottenham Hotspur (Home), September 1994 | |
| | League Cup 2nd Round, 1st Leg | 3-6 |
| 438. | v. Derby County (Home), January 1982 | |
| | Division Two | 6-1 |
| 439. | v. Everton (Home), February 1984 | |
| | Division One | 4-4 |
| 440. | v. Bradford City (Home), December 1989 | |
| | Division Two | 7-2 |

## DAVID JAMES

441. 1970
442. Millwall
443. Mexico
444. Colin Lee
445. Player of the Year award
446. He was the youngest ever Watford player to win the award
447. Aston Villa
448. 2000 (v. Italy, away, England lost 1-0)
449. Harry Redknapp
450. Liverpool

## LEAGUE GOALSCORERS - 1

| 451. | Tommy Barnett | 144 |
| 452. | Dennis Bond | 37 |
| 453. | Bill Devan | 33 |
| 454. | Roy Brown | 40 |
| 455. | Maurice Cook | 68 |
| 456. | Luther Blissett | 139 |
| 457. | John Barnes | 65 |
| 458. | Harry Lowe | 41 |
| 459. | Fred Pagnam | 67 |
| 460. | Wilf Rostron | 22 |

## 1960s

461.  6 pence
462.  3rd
463.  Ron Burgess
464.  George Harris
465.  Micky Walker
466.  Ken Furphy
467.  Cliff Holton
468.  Bill McGarry
469.  Grimsby Town
470.  1968/1969

## NIGEL GIBBS

471.  Defender (Right Back)
472.  3
473.  1965
474.  Wolverhampton Wanderers
475.  West Bromwich Albion
476.  Graham Taylor
477.  Darlington
478.  2
479.  His knee
480.  England

## PREMIER LEAGUE 2006/2007

481.  Aidy Boothroyd
482.  Middlesbrough
483.  Marlon King
484.  Charlton Athletic and Tottenham Hotspur
485.  Ashley Young
486.  Ben Foster
487.  Ashley Young
488.  29
489.  Chris Powell
490.  Will Hoskins and Lee Williamson

## LEAGUE POSITIONS - 1

| 491. | 2005/2006 | 3rd  |
|------|-----------|------|
| 492. | 2003/2004 | 16th |
| 493. | 2001/2002 | 14th |
| 494. | 1999/2000 | 20th |
| 495. | 1997/1998 | 1st  |

| 496. | 1995/1996 | 23rd |
|------|-----------|------|
| 497. | 1993/1994 | 19th |
| 498. | 1991/1992 | 10th |
| 499. | 1989/1990 | 15th |
| 500. | 1987/1988 | 20th |

## STEVE TERRY

501. 1962
502. Sunderland
503. Defender (Centre Back)
504. 160
505. Graham Taylor
506. 14
507. True
508. Northampton Town
509. England (Amateur)
510. Hull City

## MATCH OF THE YEAR - 2

| 511. | Watford record their highest home attendance of 34,099 v. Manchester United in the FA Cup | 1969 |
|------|-----|------|
| 512. | Watford participate for the first time in European competition | 1983 |
| 513. | Dave Bassett is appointed as manager | 1987 |
| 514. | Graham Simpson joins the Watford board | 1999 |
| 515. | Watford beats Sockport County 4-1 in the 3rd round of the FA Cup | 2007 |
| 516. | Dixie Hale signs for Watford | 1967 |
| 517. | Aidy Boothroyd is appointed as manager | 2005 |
| 518. | Brian Talbot leaves Vicarage Road and joins Stoke City | 1986 |
| 519. | Marlon King scores his first goal for the Hornets | 2005 |
| 520. | Bill Findlay is appointed as manager | 1937 |

## CLIFF HOLTON

521. 1929
522. 144
523. Neil McBain
524. Centre Forward
525. 48
526. Arsenal
527. Crystal Palace

528.    Ken Furphy
529.    Northampton Town
530.    1966

## LEAGUE APPEARANCES - 1

| | | |
|---|---|---|
| 531. | Bill Jannings | 80 (13) |
| 532. | Roger Joslyn | 178 (4) |
| 533. | Dennis Bond | 271 (1) |
| 534. | Luther Blissett | 335 (38) |
| 535. | John Barnes | 232 (1) |
| 536. | Kenny Jackett | 330 (7) |
| 537. | Steve Sherwood | 211 |
| 538. | Paul Wilkinson | 135 (1) |
| 539. | Taffy Davies | 283 |
| 540. | Duncan Welbourne | 404 (7) |

## WATFORD V. ARSENAL

541.    Luther Blissett and John Barnes
542.    John Barnes
543.    Kenny Jackett and Luther Blissett
544.    1-0 to Arsenal
545.    1988 (April)
546.    1-0 to Watford (winning at Highbury)
547.    True: 3-0 (home) and 2-0 (away)
548.    Graham Taylor: April 1983
549.    1906
550.    Luther Blissett and Gary Porter

## MARLON KING

551.    1980
552.    Preston North End
553.    Plymouth Argyle
554.    Wolverhampton Wanderers
555.    West Ham United
556.    Jamaica
557.    Aidy Boothroyd
558.    Gillingham
559.    9
560.    Barnet

## POT LUCK - 1

561.    Bertie Mee

562.    John Ward
563.    Herald & Post
564.    Iveco
565.    £9.50
566.    Eagle Express
567.    Ron Burgess
568.    Len Goulden
569.    Wolverhampton Wanderers (FA Cup 1st round replay)
570.    1977/1978

## KENNY JACKETT
571.    1962
572.    Wales
573.    31
574.    25
575.    3
576.    Sunderland
577.    Graham Taylor
578.    True
579.    5
580.    Swansea City

## THE FA CUP - 1
581.    Malky Mackay (2), Tommy Smith and Moses Ashikodi
582.    Luther Blissett
583.    Ross Jenkins
584.    Colchester United
585.    Chelsea
586.    Gifton Noel-Williams
587.    Andy Hessenthaler
588.    Wimbledon (Milton Keynes Dons)
589.    Guildford City
590.    Glenn Roeder

## STEVE PERRYMAN
591.    1990
592.    Colin Lee
593.    Coventry City
594.    0-0
595.    Plymouth Argyle
596.    20th
597.    Tottenham Hotspur

598.     Brentford
599.     Andy Hessenthaler
600.     1993

## ROSS JENKINS
601.     London
602.     Crystal Palace
603.     George Kirby
604.     Centre Forward
605.     Washington Diplomats
606.     29
607.     118
608.     2
609.     339: 312 (27)
610.     1975/1976 and 1978/1979

## PLAYER NATIONALITIES - 1
611.     Marlon King          Jamaican
612.     Tamas Priskin        Hungarian
613.     Albert Jarrett       Sierra Leonean
614.     Danny Shittu         Nigerian
615.     Jay DeMerit          American
616.     Malky Mackay         Scottish
617.     Tommy Smith          English
618.     Clarke Carlisle      English
619.     Damien Francis       Jamaican
620.     Mart Poom            Estonian

## TONY COTON
621.     1984
622.     Everton
623.     Birmingham City
624.     £300,000
625.     Graham Taylor
626.     Manchester City
627.     1961
628.     235
629.     Manchester United
630.     Goalkeeper

## WHERE DID THEY COME FROM? - 1
631.     Gerry Armstrong          Tottenham Hotspur

| 632. | Maurice Johnston | Partick Thistle |
|------|------------------|-----------------|
| 633. | Brian Talbot | Arsenal |
| 634. | Peter Kennedy | Notts County |
| 635. | Tommy Mooney | Southend United |
| 636. | Malky Mackay | West Ham United |
| 637. | Damien Francis | Wigan Athletic |
| 638. | Chris Powell | Charlton Athletic |
| 639. | Jordan Stewart | Leicester City |
| 640. | Nathan Ellington | West Bromwich Albion |

## PAUL ROBINSON

641. 1978
642. Robbo
643. Luton Town
644. Graham Taylor
645. Defender (Left)
646. Fulham
647. Crewe Alexandra
648. 3
649. West Bromwich Albion
650. Milton Keynes Dons, Coventry City and Preston North End

## WATFORD V. TOTTENHAM HOTSPUR

651. Luther Blissett
652. 0-0
653. Richard Johnson
654. 6-8 (3-6 at home and 3-2 away)
655. The FA Cup (a 4-1 defeat)
656. Maurice Johnston
657. 1-0 to Tottenham Hotspur
658. Graham Taylor
659. Allan Smart
660. Les Taylor

## LEAGUE GOALSCORERS - 2

| 661. | Charlie White | 81 |
|------|---------------|-----|
| 662. | Peter Turner | 20 |
| 663. | Freddie Bunce | 34 |
| 664. | Stewart Scullion | 49 |
| 665. | Charlie Hare | 23 |
| 666. | Ian Bolton | 28 |
| 667. | Ross Jenkins | 118 |

| 668. | Paul Wilkinson | 51 |
| 669. | Dai Ward | 31 |
| 670. | Wally Eames | 11 |

## DUNCAN WELBOURNE

671. Scunthorpe
672. 1965/1966
673. 411: 404 (7)
674. Bill McGarry
675. Grimsby Town
676. 22
677. Blackburn Rovers (Away) and Bolton Wanderers (Away)
678. 1964/1965
679. Hull City (Home)
680. 1974

## PLAYER NATIONALITIES - 2

| 681. | Hameur Bouazza | Algerian |
| 682. | Gary Porter | English |
| 683. | Gavin Mahon | English |
| 684. | Pat Jennings | Northern Irish |
| 685. | Tom Jones | Welsh |
| 686. | Toumani Diagouraga | French |
| 687. | Joe McLaughlin | Scottish |
| 688. | Claude Seanla | Ivorian |
| 689. | Joel Grant | Jamaican |
| 690. | Kevin Phillips | English |

## PROMOTION TO THE PREMIER LEAGUE - 2005/2006

691. Leeds United
692. Crystal Palace
693. 3rd
694. Aidy Boothroyd
695. 22
696. Marlon King
697. Chris Eagles, Marlon King (2) and Hameur Bouazza
698. Darius Henderson
699. Ipswich Town
700. Burnley

## ROBERT PAGE

701. Wales

702.    Sheffield Wednesday
703.    Defender (Central)
704.    Birmingham City
705.    Steve Perryman
706.    1974
707.    Coventry City
708.    Sheffield Wednesday
709.    Preston North End
710.    Sheffield United

## DIVISION THREE CHAMPIONS - 1968/1969

711.    Barry Endean
712.    27
713.    Swindon Town
714.    Ken Furphy
715.    Gillingham
716.    Mansfield Town
717.    Keith Eddy, Tom Walley and Duncan Welbourne
718.    1-0 to Watford
719.    Rodney Green
720.    19

## WILF ROSTRON

721.    Sunderland
722.    1982/1983 and 1983/1984
723.    3
724.    3
725.    Queens Park Rangers
726.    22
727.    Leicester City
728.    Leicester City
729.    He was suspended
730.    Sheffield Wednesday

## PLAY-OFF WINNERS - 1998/1999

731.    Bolton
732.    Birmingham City
733.    Graham Taylor
734.    5th
735.    Gifton Noel-Williams
736.    Alec Chamberlain and Peter Kennedy
737.    Peter Kennedy

738. Sunderland
739. Queens Park Rangers
740. Bristol City and Swindon Town

## RESULTS - 2

| | | |
|---|---|---|
| 741. | v. Sunderland (Away), April 1972 | |
| | Division Two | 0-5 |
| 742. | v. Barrow (Away), December 1978 | |
| | Division Three | 4-1 |
| 743. | v. Crewe Alexandra (Home), April 1969 | |
| | Division Three | 4-0 |
| 744. | v. Everton (Home), September 1984 | |
| | Division One | 4-5 |
| 745. | v. Crewe Alexandra (Home), October 1977 | |
| | Division Four | 5-2 |
| 746. | v. Doncaster Rovers (Home), March 1977 | |
| | Division Four | 5-1 |
| 747. | v. Bury (Home), January 1979 | |
| | Division Three | 3-3 |
| 748. | v. Blackburn Rovers (Away), December 1992 | |
| | League Cup 4th Round | 1-6 |
| 749. | v. Peterborough United (Away), April 1994 | |
| | Division One | 4-3 |
| 750. | v. Aston Villa (Away), January 2007 | |
| | Premier League | 0-2 |

## GARY PORTER

751. 1966
752. 396: 358 (38)
753. Graham Taylor
754. Bolton Wanderers
755. Luther Blissett
756. England
757. 46
758. 1985/1986
759. Midfield
760. Walsall

## LEAGUE APPEARANCES - 2

| | | |
|---|---|---|
| 761. | Stewart Scullion | 304 (8) |
| 762. | Skilly Williams | 323 |
| 763. | Ken Furphy | 95 (6) |

| 764. | Johnny Williams | 371 (3) |
| 765. | David Bardsley | 97 (3) |
| 766. | Pat Rice | 112 |
| 767. | Frank McPherson | 94 |
| 768. | Vic O'Brien | 179 |
| 769. | Arthur Daniels | 136 |
| 770. | Jack Moran | 100 |

## ROGER JOSLYN

771. Colchester
772. 1974
773. Gillingham
774. 182: 178 (4)
775. Scunthorpe United (Home), Rochdale (Away) and Exeter City (Home)
776. 17
777. 2
778. Doncaster Rovers
779. Mike Keen
780. Reading

## TOMMY MOONEY

781. Southend United
782. 1994
783. Sunderland
784. 1971
785. 22: 19 League, 2 League Cup, 1 FA Cup
786. Liverpool
787. Southend United
788. Norwich City
789. 6
790. Birmingham City

## POT LUCK - 2

791. Jack Petchey
792. Cliff Holton
793. Ken Furphy
794. Blaupunkt
795. Cassio Road
796. Saracens
797. Elton John and Graham Taylor
798. The Golden Boys

799.     Keith Burkinshaw
800.     1999

## ALEC CHAMBERLAIN
801.     Goalkeeper
802.     Luton Town
803.     Charlton Athletic
804.     1964
805.     Graham Taylor
806.     Crewe Alexandra
807.     Sunderland
808.     1
809.     4
810.     Colchester United

## WHERE DID THEY GO? - 2
811.     John Barnes                    Liverpool
812.     Gifton Noel-Williams           Stoke City
813.     Michel Ngonge                  Queens Park Rangers
814.     Darren Bazeley                 Walsall
815.     Allan Nielsen                  Herfolge
816.     Robert Page                    Sheffield United
817.     Neal Ardley                    Cardiff City
818.     Marcus Gayle                   Brentford
819.     Brynjar Gunnarsson             Reading
820.     Keith Millen                   Bristol City

## GIANLUCA VIALLI
821.     2001
822.     Graham Taylor
823.     Chelsea
824.     Manchester City
825.     14th
826.     Cremonese, Sampdoria and Juventus
827.     Rotherham
828.     Italian
829.     59
830.     Ray Lewington

## COMINGS AND GOINGS - 1
831.     James Chambers
832.     Marcus Gayle

833.  Oldham Athletic
834.  Willie Falconer
835.  Steve Morrow
836.  Norwich City
837.  Roger Willis
838.  Colin West
839.  Ramon Vega
840.  Walsall

## AIDY BOOTHROYD
841.  2005
842.  Hearts
843.  Defender
844.  English
845.  26
846.  Peterborough United
847.  Championship Play-Off Winners 2006
848.  Leeds United
849.  Ray Lewington
850.  1971

## DIVISION TWO CHAMPIONS - 1997/1998
851.  Graham Taylor
852.  Peter Kennedy
853.  Bristol City and Grimsby Town
854.  Richard Johnson, Dai Thomas and Peter Kennedy (2)
855.  Fulham
856.  Gifton Noel-Williams and Jason Lee
857.  Ronny Rosenthal
858.  Southend United
859   Burnley
860.  88

## BIG WINS - 2
861.  v. West Bromwich Albion (Home)
      Division 1, August 1985                          5-1
862.  v. Chelsea (Away)
      Division 1, May 1986                             5-1
863.  v. Sheffield United (Home)
      FA Cup 3rd Round, January 1985                   5-0
864.  v. Wolverhampton Wanderers (Away)
      Division 1, December 1983                        5-0

| 865. | v. Sunderland (Home) | |
| | Division 1, September 1982 | 8-0 |
| 866. | v. Brighton & Hove Albion (Home) | |
| | Division 1, November 1982 | 4-1 |
| 867. | v. Tranmere Rovers (Home) | |
| | Division 3, September 1978 | 4-0 |
| 868. | v. Southport (Home) | |
| | Division 3, March 1974 | 4-0 |
| 869. | v. Scunthorpe United (Home) | |
| | Division 3, March 1973 | 5-1 |
| 870. | v. Portsmouth (Home) | |
| | Division 2, October 1969 | 4-0 |

## WATFORD V. WEST HAM UNITED

871. Ross Jenkins and Kenny Jackett
872. 1-1
873. Nigel Callaghan and Gerry Armstrong
874. 4-2 to Watford
875. 1-0 to West Ham United
876. 5-0 to Watford
877. True: 0-2 (Home) and 1-2 (Away)
878. Luther Blissett
879. 1982 (1982/1983 season)
880. 2-1 to Watford

## NIGEL CALLAGHAN

881. 1962
882. Preston North End
883. Singapore
884. 1
885. Leeds United
886. Queens Park Rangers (Home), Nottingham Forest (Away), Manchester City (Home) and Oxford United (Home)
887. England
888. 42
889. Southampton
890. Derby County

## DIVISION THREE RUNNERS-UP - 1978/1979

891. Shrewsbury Town
892. 83
893. Hull City

894.    John Stirk and Ross Jenkins
895.    Graham Taylor
896.    Lincoln City
897.    20
898.    Ross Jenkins
899.    20 pence
900.    24

## FA CUP SEMI-FINALISTS - 1987

901.    Tottenham Hotspur
902.    Arsenal
903.    3-1 to Watford
904.    Luther Blissett
905.    Mark Falco
906.    Gary Plumley
907.    Luther Blissett
908.    Chelsea
909.    Luther Blissett
910.    Walsall

## HOW MUCH DID I COST?

| | | |
|---|---|---|
| 911. | Gerry Armstrong | £250,000 |
| 912. | Pat Jennings | £6,000 |
| 913. | Steve Sherwood | £3,000 |
| 914. | Tony Coton | £300,000 |
| 915. | Lee Nogan | £300,000 |
| 916. | John McClelland | £225,000 |
| 917. | Perry Suckling | Free Transfer |
| 918. | Brian Talbot | £150,000 |
| 919. | Duncan Welbourne | £1,300 |
| 920. | Devon White | £100,000 |

## FA CUP FINAL - 1984

921.    Everton
922.    Graham Taylor
923.    2-0 to Everton
924.    Graeme Sharp and Andy Gray
925.    Steve Sherwood, David Bardsley, Neil Price, Les Taylor,
        Steve Terry, Lee Sinnott, Nigel Callaghan, Mo Johnston,
        George Reilly, Kenny Jackett and John Barnes
926.    Plymouth Argyle
927.    Charlton Athletic

928.    Wembley Stadium
929.    Luton Town
930.    Birmingham City

## LEAGUE POSITIONS - 2
931.    1985/1986          12th
932.    1983/1984          11th
933.    1981/1982          2nd
934.    1979/1980          18th
935.    1977/1978          1st
936.    1975/1976          8th
937.    1973/1974          7th
938.    1971/1972          22nd
939.    1969/1970          19th
940.    1967/1968          6th

## DIVISION ONE RUNNERS-UP - 1982/1983
941.    Liverpool
942.    22
943.    Sunderland
944.    John Barnes, Wilf Rostron and Steve Sherwood
945.    Jimmy Gilligan
946.    November: 4 wins: Tottenham Hotspur (Away), Stoke City (Home),
        Brighton & Hove Albion (Home) and Arsenal (Away)
947.    Gerry Armstrong
948.    Elton John
949.    Southampton
950.    Luther Blissett

## COMINGS AND GOINGS - 2
951.    Les Ferdinand
952.    Neil Cox
953.    Doncaster Rovers
954.    Xavier Gravelaine
955.    Carl Fletcher
956.    Bruce Dyer
957.    Espen Baardsen
958.    Chesterfield
959.    Bradford City
960.    Paul Jones

## JOHN McCLELLAND

961.    1955
962.    Northern Ireland
963.    1984
964.    Rangers
965.    Liverpool
966.    3
967.    Leeds United
968.    53
969.    Newcastle United
970.    Defender (Central)

## WHERE DID THEY COME FROM? - 2

| 971. | Darius Henderson | Gillingham |
| 972. | Bruce Dyer | Barnsley |
| 973. | Neil Cox | Bolton Wanderers |
| 974. | Johann Gudmundsson | IB Keflavik |
| 975. | Jason Lee | Nottingham Forest |
| 976. | Steve Palmer | Ipswich Town |
| 977. | Ronny Rosenthal | Tottenham Hotspur |
| 978. | Pat Rice | Arsenal |
| 979. | Tommy Smith | Derby County |
| 980. | Paul Furlong | Coventry City |

## HEIDAR HELGUSON

981.    Iceland
982.    Graham Taylor
983.    Liverpool
984.    6
985.    Liverpool, Bradford City, West Ham United, Arsenal, Manchester United and Coventry City
986.    Lillestrom
987.    Barnsley
988.    West Ham United
989.    20
990.    Fulham

## POT LUCK - 3

991.    2002
992.    Keith Mercer
993.    David Underwood
994.    319

995.    *Peter Taylor*
996.    *Tony Geidmintis*
997.    *WD18 0ER*
998.    *Dai Ward*
999.    *Scott Loach*
1000.   *1982*

# sense
TOUCHING PEOPLE'S LIVES
## ABOUT 'SENSE'

## Our services
Sense has a worldwide reputation for its expertise in working with deafblind people. We also work with people with single sensory impairments and a wide range of other difficulties - including physical disabilities, learning disabilities, and challenging behaviour.

## What we offer
Sense works with a wide age range, from babies who have just been diagnosed to older people. We also offer training and other services related to deafblindness.

## Our services:
* offer a flexible person-centred approach
* are built around the needs and talents of each individual
* offer disabled people of all ages the chance to develop their potential to the full
* promote choice and respect for the individual
* enable deafblind people to play their full part in the life of the community
* are well-run, accountable and cost-effective.

## CONTACT DETAILS:
Sense's head office is based at:
11-13 Clifton Terrace, Finsbury Park, London, N4 3SR
Tel: 0845 127 0060    Fax: 0845 127 0061
E-mail: info@sense.org.uk    Website: www.sense.org.uk

134

## ALSO BY CHRIS COWLIN...

# THE OFFICIAL NORWICH CITY FOOTBALL CLUB QUIZ BOOK

**Foreword by Bryan Gunn**
**ISBN: 1-904444-80-6**
**Price: £7.99**

*£1 from every copy of the book sold will go to
'The Norwich City Football Club Historical Trust'.*

*Will you be singing like a Canary as you fly with ease through this book's 1,000 challenging quiz questions about Norwich City Football Club, or will you have flown the Nest too soon and come crashing to the ground spitting feathers? Covering all aspects of the club's history, including top goalscorers, transfers, managers, Cup competitions, League positions, awards, legendary players and nationalities, it will push to the limit even the most ardent aficionados' knowledge of their favourite team.*

*With a fitting foreword by the legendary Bryan Gunn, this book is guaranteed to trigger fond recollections of all the nail-biting matches and colourful characters that have shaped the club over the years, as well as providing a wealth of interesting facts and figures with which to impress your friends and family.*

*"How much do you know about this great club? This excellent book will help you to discover the answer to that question and to many more." - **Chris Woods***

*"Reckon you're a Norwich City fan? Do you know your Gunn's from your Huckerby's? Prove yourself with The Official Norwich City Football Club Quiz Book." - **Darren Huckerby***

*"An absolute must for all die hard Canaries fans. I really enjoyed answering the questions from the promotion year 1986, which I played my part in."*
*- **Steve Bruce***

# TO ORDER YOUR COPY PLEASE CONTACT NORWICH FC

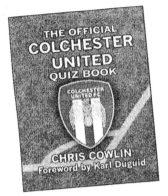

## ALSO BY CHRIS COWLIN (AND PETER MILES)...

# THE SOUTHEND UNITED QUIZ BOOK

### Foreword by Frank Dudley
### ISBN: 1-904444-91-1
### Price: £5.99

*Will you be a Shrimper with a record catch as you reel in the answers to the 800 tricky questions in this quiz book about Southend United Football Club, or will you be singing the Blues as you bemoan the one, or more, that got away?*

*Your knowledge about all aspects of the club since its formation will be tested to the limit, from memorable managers and players to transfer fees, opponents, scores, awards and all the unforgettable competitions and matches that have kept fans on the edge of their seats throughout the club's long history.*

*With a fitting foreword by Frank Dudley, this quiz book is brimming with interesting facts and figures and is guaranteed to provide hours of entertainment, reminiscing and discussion for fans of the club.*

*"If you think you know everything about Southend United - think again!"*
**- Glenn Speller, BBC Radio Essex 103.5 & 95.3 FM (Sports Producer)**

*"Having read Chris Cowlin's other quiz books I knew to expect a thoroughly researched and detailled book - and I certainly wasn't disappointed. Chris is certainly top of the league when it comes to football trivia!"*
**- Stephen Lee, Anglia Television (Presenter)**

## TO ORDER YOUR COPY PLEASE PHONE: 01255 428500

*ALSO BY CHRIS COWLIN...*

# CELEBRITIES' FAVOURITE FOOTBALL TEAMS

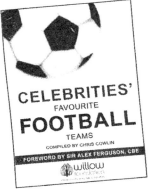

Foreword by Sir Alex Ferguson CBE
ISBN: 1-904444-84-9
Price: £6.99

*All of the author's royalties will be donated
to 'The Willow Foundation' charity.*

special days for seriously ill young adults

*We all like to delve into the minds and lives of our beloved celebrity figures, but this fascinating read is not celebrity gossip, it comes straight from the horse's mouth to reveal all you ever wanted to know about celebrities' favourite football teams and players.*

*With a fitting Foreword by footballing legend Sir Alex Ferguson CBE, this book is a must-read for football fans who wish to know which celebrity is a fellow aficionado of their club, or perhaps a supporter of 'the enemy', as well as for the rest of the population, who just love to know what makes our celebrities tick.*

*And it is also a must-buy, as all royalties from the sale of this book will be donated to The Willow Foundation, a charity set up by the legendary Bob Wilson and his wife Megs in 1999 to enable seriously ill young adults to enjoy the treat of a 'Special Day' with family and friends.*

*"Sporting heroes of the stars revealed...
a really fascinating insight!"*
**- Neil Greenfield, Tottenham Journal**

*"A fun read! Not only do you get a good read, but you're also donating to a good cause."*
**- Vince Cooper, The League Magazine**

## TO ORDER YOUR COPY
## PLEASE PHONE: 01255 428500

# REVIEWS

"1,000 questions from the rich history of Watford FC to test the knowledge of everyone from the devoted fan to the casual supporter. Having tested the book myself on friends and family, their reaction makes me more than happy to recommend the book as an ideal addition to a Watford supporter's bookcase."
**- www.hornethistory.com**

"Clearly this quiz book has been thoroughly researched by a passionate football fan."
**- www.hertfordshire.com**

"What a test for any hornet fan!"
**- www.eastmidshorns.150m.com**

"Reckon you're a true Hornets fan? From Rose and Crown Meadow to Vicarage Road, from Luther Blisset to John Barnes - it's all in The Official Watford Quiz Book..."
**- www.4thegame.com**

"An essential purchase for all Hornets fans, this book fills the void at home watching the match with your friends and family, on the bus going to that Tuesday night match up North, or even just to browse through and top up your knowledge of Watford Football Club. Highly recommended by Football Heaven."
**- www.footballheaven.net**

"The Official Watford Quiz Book will provide hours of entertainment for any Hornets fan. I love a bit of trivia and now I can entertain my fellow fans in the Rookery with facts and figures that they thought I would never need but now love to know.
**- Martin Booth, Watford Observer**